P9-CEI-686

World War II Love Stories

MY
SERVICE DIARY
V
CLOSE COVER BEFORE STRIKING MATCH

WORLD WAR II
Love Stories

At a time of global calamity,
the true stories of 14 couples
who found love

GILL PAUL

Introduction by
Andrew Roberts

METRO BOOKS
NEW YORK

For William Boag Paul, the uncle I never met, who was one of the last men out of Dunkirk; and his son Jim, who is one of the nicest men I know.

METRO BOOKS
New York

An Imprint of Sterling Publishing
387 Park Avenue South
New York, NY 10016

METRO BOOKS and the distinctive Metro Books logo are trademarks of Sterling Publishing Co., Inc.

This book was conceived, designed, and produced by Ivy Press

Ivy Press

210 High Street, Lewes, East Sussex, BN7 2NS, UK

Creative Director Peter Bridgewater

Publisher Susan Kelly

Art Director Wayne Blades

Senior Editors Jacqui Sayers & Jayne Ansell

Designer Andrew Milne

Picture Researcher Katie Greenwood

ISBN 978-1-4351-4786-7

Library of Congress Cataloging-in-Publication Data

For information about custom editions, special sales, and premium and corporate purchases, please contact Sterling Special Sales at 800-805-5489 or specialsales@sterlingpublishing.com.

Manufactured in China

Color origination by Ivy Press Reprographics

2 4 6 8 10 9 7 5 3 1

www.sterlingpublishing.com

CONTENTS

Introduction – 6

Coco Chanel & Hans von Dincklage – 20
French fashion designer Coco Chanel's affair with an aristocratic German attaché was fiercely controversial and led to her arrest at the war's end.

William & Kathleen Anderson – 32
William and Kathleen's unyielding love for each other helped him to survive imprisonment in Colditz.

Bill & Norma Kay Moore – 44
Romantic Bill went AWOL so he could spend his first wedding anniversary with his wife, Norma.

Desmond Paul & Louisa Henry – 56
Desmond and Louisa's love blossomed after a chance encounter, and this love would save his life on two occasions.

Étienne & Violette Szabo – 68
Married barely a month after they met, Étienne and Violette tragically had very little time together.

Charley & Jean Paul – 80
Charley and Jean's deep love helped her to survive the tough realities of life on a Tobique reserve in the wilds of Canada.

Dwight D. Eisenhower & Kay Summersby – 92
Despite his elevated position and a wife back home, Dwight clearly had strong feelings for Kay.

Roger & Rosemarie Williams – 104
Roger and Rosemarie met in northern Germany as the Russian army approached and the Iron Curtain split her family in two.

Allen Dulles & Mary Bancroft – 116
Mary's affair with Allen, a spy, was unconventional, thrilling and potentially dangerous.

Hudson & Betty Turner – 128
Betty wrote 300 letters to GI Hudson and always hoped he'd come back to marry her.

Bob & Rosie Norwalk – 140
Bob was unhappily married and when he met cheerful, friendly Rosie he knew he had found the true love of his life.

Raymond & Lucie Aubrac – 152
Raymond and Lucie were intrepid members of the Resistance, willing to risk all for their country's freedom.

Hedley & Dorrit Nash – 164
Hedley and Dorrit were opposites in every way, except the fact that they were both outsiders in a foreign land.

Roy Sather & Pill Denman – 176
Roy and Pill had an intense Pacific island romance, and both hoped that they would spend the rest of their lives together.

Index – 188
Acknowledgments – 190
Picture Credits – 191

I WILL
GIVE POLES
A LESSON
-HITLER
EVENING
STANDARD
HITLER
INVADES
POLAND
EVENING
NEWS
POLAND
INVADED
-OFFICIAL
THE
STAR
DANZIG
GOES TO
GERMANY
BOLS

Introduction

by Andrew Roberts

The Nazi Threat

When Adolf Hitler was appointed Chancellor of Germany on January 30, 1933, few people predicted that this event would lead to a second world war by the end of the decade.

World War I—the Great War—had ended less than 15 years earlier, and no one believed that someone who had himself served in the trenches of the Western Front would seek to provoke another conflict on such a terrible scale. Yet the program of Hitler's National Socialist ("Nazi") Party was one of pure aggression, born of resentment at Germany's ill-treatment at the Versailles Conference that had formally brought World War I to an end. Germany rearmed, and within three years her industrial and military might allowed Hitler to force the Western Powers—mainly Britain and France, along with the United States—into a series of humiliating diplomatic defeats.

Hitler remilitarized the Rhineland in March 1936 (flouting the terms of the Versailles Treaty), forced Austria into Anschluss (union) with his Third Reich in March 1938, and threatened to invade the German-speaking areas of Czechoslovakia (called the Sudetenland) in September of that same year, while also

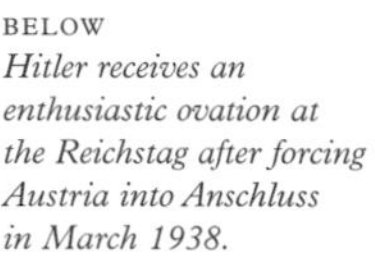

BELOW
Hitler receives an enthusiastic ovation at the Reichstag after forcing Austria into Anschluss in March 1938.

supporting the efforts of two fellow fascists: Francisco Franco in the Spanish Civil War, and Benito Mussolini in the invasion of Abyssinia (modern-day Ethiopia). Meanwhile, Germany withdrew from the League of Nations, the ineffectual forerunner of the United Nations.

ABOVE
"The alliance between Italy and German is not only between two states or two armies ... but between two peoples." Speech by Mussolini in Rome, February 23, 1941.

In each of these cases, and in many other areas of diplomacy, Britain and France permitted the Nazis to get what they wanted, believing that Germany had been ill-treated by the victorious powers at Versailles. They hoped that by appeasing the Third Reich, its anger and bitterness would diminish. Instead, the lesson Hitler drew from his successes was that the Western democracies were inherently feeble and would let him get away with further territorial inclusions. In March 1939, he invaded those parts of Czechoslovakia—principally Bohemia and Moravia—that were not German-speaking, while the government-controlled German press began making threats against Poland.

On March 31, 1939, the British prime minister, Neville Chamberlain, told Parliament of his pledge to the Polish Government that if the Germans invaded Poland, Britain would immediately go to war on her behalf. It was more of a gesture, a bluff, than a workable guarantee, as there was little that Britain could practically do to protect Poland if Hitler decided to attack. Then, on August 22, 1939, in one of the most cynical diplomatic coups in history, the Nazi foreign minister, Joachim von Ribbentrop, traveled to Moscow to conclude a non-aggression pact with his Soviet opposite number, Vyacheslav Molotov, the following day. Thus Poland was to be divided between the two totalitarian powers, Nazi and Communist, in a deal that would ensure the outbreak of war a matter of days later. The hope of world peace would soon be dashed.

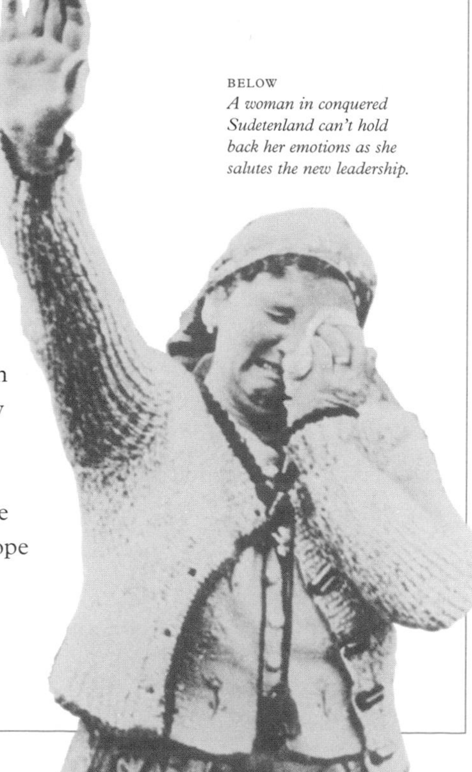

BELOW
A woman in conquered Sudetenland can't hold back her emotions as she salutes the new leadership.

Europe Overwhelmed

World War II began shortly after dawn on Friday, September 1, 1939, when two German Army groups thrust eastward, deep into Poland. Supported by Junkers Ju87 "Stuka" dive bombers, and employing the tactic of Blitzkrieg, or "lightning war," the Wehrmacht raced forward, enveloping and capturing Polish forces that had been placed too far west to be of defensive use.

What happened next was, well, very little. The "Phony War'" or "Sitzkrieg," lasted seven months as the Nazis occupied Poland and moved their forces northward and westward, but there was no fighting on any western front. The war at sea, however, was fought aggressively on both sides.

These months of uneasy waiting ended suddenly on April 9, 1940, when Hitler covered his northern flank by simultaneously invading Denmark and Norway. British and French expeditionary forces were rushed to the Norwegian coast to try to contest the German invasion, and some moved further inland, but they were pushed back and eventually forced to evacuate altogether on May 3rd. This humiliation brought down Chamberlain's government after a tumultuous debate in the House of Commons, and on May 10, 1940, Winston Churchill became prime minister. Three days later, in his first appearance in the Commons in that role, he warned the British people to expect nothing but "blood, toil, tears, and sweat," in the first of many morale-boosting speeches of his wartime premiership.

BELOW
A group of children whose house was destroyed during the Blitz: East London, September 1940.

Yet more strategic disasters would follow Norway as, on the very day that Churchill took office, Hitler unleashed his Blitzkrieg on the Low Countries and France. Through a brilliant naval operation, supported by brave Royal Air Force (RAF) sorties against the Luftwaffe, no fewer than 224,000 British and 95,000 French troops were evacuated from the beaches of Dunkirk and other ports, evading what had looked like inevitable capture. Soon afterward, France, led by General de Gaulle, appealed to Hitler for an armistice, and on June 22nd, a peace treaty was signed.

The undisputed master of the Continent, Hitler began drafting plans to invade and subjugate Great Britain. To achieve this, he needed command of the skies, and thus it fell to Hermann Göring, commander-in-chief of the Luftwaffe, to set in motion the aerial struggle that became known as the Battle of Britain. From July to the first half of September 1940, the Luftwaffe fought with the RAF for supremacy of the skies. Famously, the RAF defeated the stronger force, so that by the end of October, the Luftwaffe had lost a significant amount of its fighting strength.

The bombing of London and many other British cities after September 7, 1940, in what is now called the Blitz, was to cost the lives of nearly 60,000 British civilians. It brought the war home to ordinary Britons in a way that the overflying Zeppelins of World War I had not really succeeded in doing.

BELOW
On Sunday, September 29, 1940, as incendiary devices rained down on London, Churchill gave orders that St Paul's Cathedral must be saved at all costs for the sake of the country's morale.

BRITAIN'S WAR LEADER

Winston Churchill had long been opposed to Chamberlain's policy of appeasing Hitler, so he wasn't first choice for a wartime cabinet role, but nine months into the war it was recognized that they required his military experience and he was appointed first lord of the Admiralty. On May 8, 1940, the House of Commons began to debate the country's war strategy, and on May 10th, when Hitler invaded the Low Countries and France, Chamberlain had no choice but to resign. Lord Halifax declined to take over and Churchill stepped up and rallied the nation with his inspiring rhetoric.

At the Borders of Europe and Beyond

Although the RAF's Bomber Command responded by bombing Germany, and the Royal Navy blockaded Germany and attempted to sink raider battleships and U-boats, for a while after the Battle of Britain there was nowhere for the Allies and the Wehrmacht to clash on land, since the Axis powers controlled the European Continent, and thus any attempted invasion was judged to be suicidal. But in Libya, Egypt, the Sudan, Ethiopia, and along the North African littoral, the British Army under General Wavell was able to score several significant victories over Marshal Graziani's Italian troops, despite being heavily outnumbered.

These advances were not to last, however, as in February 1941, Churchill ordered forces to be diverted to protect Greece, just as the brilliant German commander General Erwin Rommel arrived in Tripoli to take command of the German Afrika Korps. Having also suborned Romania and Hungary onto its own side, on April 6th, Germany invaded Yugoslavia, which fell in a mere 11 days. Soon afterward, British forces had to be evacuated from Greece to Crete, only for a German force of some 22,000 airborne troops under General Kurt Student to stage a daring landing on the island. After eight days of fighting, here, too, the British were forced to leave.

BELOW
Conditions in the desert were harsh, with fierce daytime temperatures and severe cold at night, as well as sandstorms that could blow in at any moment. Here a German bomb lands close to an American truck.

The war was not going well for the Allies, but that same month, June 1941, Hitler made a disastrous error in launching Operation Barbarossa, a surprise invasion of the USSR. This set in motion a four-year struggle between the German Führer and the Soviet dictator Josef Stalin, which would turn the tide of the war.

Meanwhile, the war in North Africa surged back and forth between Cairo in Egypt and Tobruk in Libya. Wavell was replaced by

LEFT
Russian soldiers, enduring sub-zero temperatures, defend a factory during the Battle of Stalingrad. The German officers in command wanted to win the city as a Christmas present for Hitler, but were unable to prevail.

General Claude Auchinleck, who was himself supplanted by General Bernard Montgomery. Montgomery defeated Rommel, convincingly so, in a well-planned battle at El Alamein in Libya between October 28 and November 4, 1942. On November 8th, Allied forces under the American commander General Dwight D. Eisenhower landed in French North Africa, and before long the Germans were in full retreat. Tobruk had been taken by Rommel in June, but was back in British hands just five months later.

Simultaneous with the broiling desert war, thousands of miles away on the River Volga, the Battle of Stalingrad was being contested in grim sub-zero temperatures between German and Russian armies. Here, too, German forces were finally routed, so that after four months of bitter struggle the German Sixth Army under Field Marshal Friedrich Paulus surrendered to the Red Army command. That month, Hitler bowed to the military realities and sanctioned the withdrawal westward of much of the rest of his forces, beginning a retreat that would continue until the Russians took Berlin in May 1945. Although the losses suffered by the Red Army numbered in the millions, their determination to rid the Russian motherland of the Nazi invader never wavered. Hitler had captured Stalingrad, had come within 20 miles of Moscow, and subjected Leningrad to a torturous thousand-day siege, but through all these trials the spirit of the Russian people never broke.

War in the Pacific

An error as serious as Hitler's invasion of Russia was made by Germany's ally, Imperial Japan, when on December 7, 1941, it unleashed a massive surprise attack on the American Pacific fleet as it lay at anchor at the Pearl Harbor naval base in Hawaii. The Japanese fighters, bombers, and torpedo planes succeeded in sinking four battleships, damaging four more, destroying 188 aircraft, and killing 2,403 US servicemen. What President Franklin D. Roosevelt called "a day that would live in infamy" brought the United States into the conflict. Hitler's near-lunatic decision to declare war against America four days later effectively sealed his ultimate fate.

BELOW
Roosevelt signs the declaration of war on Japan, the day after the attack on Pearl Harbor.

Between December 22 and 28, 1941, Winston Churchill visited Washington and Ottawa with his service chiefs to work with the American and Canadian governments in establishing the key stages toward achieving victory. President Roosevelt and his chief of staff, General George Marshall, eschewed the obvious response to Pearl Harbor—a massive retaliation against the immediate aggressor, Japan—to concentrate instead on a "Germany First" policy that would destroy the most powerful of the Axis dictatorships as a priority before moving on to crush Japan. The United States also agreed to make no separate peace with any Axis power and to aid Russia to the maximum extent possible, to which end the US provided 5,000 aircraft, 8,000 tanks, 51 million pairs of boots, as well as other supplies. In setting out his plans, Churchill was enormously helped by General Sir Alan Brooke, chief of the imperial general staff and one of the foremost strategic thinkers of the war.

RIGHT
The USS Shaw *takes a direct hit during the attack on Pearl Harbor. She was repaired and in use throughout the Pacific during the war.*

"Germany First," although it made good political and strategic sense, had the drawback of allowing the Japanese in the early months of 1942 to make huge advances throughout the Far East—advances characterized by dreadful cruelty to the people they conquered and to the prisoners-of-war they captured. Catastrophe for the Allies was followed by humiliation at Japanese hands. On December 10, 1941, Japanese aircraft sank HMS *Prince of Wales* and HMS *Repulse*; on Christmas Day, Hong Kong surrendered; and in January 1942, Japanese troops invaded the Dutch East Indies and Burma, and captured Kuala Lumpur, Malaysia. On February 15th, Britain suffered her greatest defeat since the American War of Independence when the great naval base of Singapore surrendered to a smaller Japanese force. The Americans were also forced out of the Philippines.

After these startling victories of late 1941 and early 1942, however, Japan became bogged down in the Far East, fought to a standstill by General Sir William Slim's Fourteenth Army in Burma and by General Douglas MacArthur in the Philippines and Admiral Paul Nimitz in the Pacific. Notable Allied victories included the battles of Kohima and Imphal, Midway (where four Japanese aircraft carriers were destroyed on a single day), Monywa and Iwo Jima, and the fall of Mandalay, Kyushu, and Okinawa. Despite so many successes, United States chiefs of staff estimated that the invasion of mainland Japan might cost the lives of up to a quarter of a million Allied servicemen. The fanatical, often suicidal, resistance the Japanese offered on island after island—and as kamikaze pilots against American ships—has convinced scholars and historians since that this prediction was probably not exaggerated.

BELOW
Five US marines and a US Navy corpsman raise the American flag on Mount Suribachi during the Battle of Iwo Jima. Three of them were subsequently killed in action.

ENIGMA CODE BREAKERS

Between the world wars, German scientists developed an Enigma machine that scrambled information with the use of three to five wheels. To decode messages, you needed to know the exact setting of these wheels. Top mathematicians at Bletchley Park working on Colossus, the world's first programmable computer, managed to break the code that the Germans believed was unbreakable. They used the intelligence sparingly so that German high command didn't realize the Enigma code had been broken, but it was especially useful in the fight against Rommel in North Africa and for destroying German U-boats that were targeting shipping in the North Atlantic to prevent supplies reaching Britain.

Europe Reclaimed

A major factor in the ultimate Allied victory was the success in April 1940 of cryptographers at Bletchley Park in Buckinghamshire in cracking the German "Enigma" military code machine. This led to an ever-increasing amount of intercepted radio messages to and from the German high command (OKW), codenamed Ultra. Having such precious advance knowledge of enemy plans would prove invaluable in various theaters of the war, but especially in the Battle of the Atlantic in 1943 once the German naval codes had also been broken.

On June 6,1944, the eyes of the world turned to the beaches of Normandy, where—after two nighttime airborne landings inland—4,000 ten-ton landing craft took six infantry divisions to five beachheads, codenamed (from west to east) Utah, Omaha, Gold, Juno, and Sword. In all, Operation Overlord on June 6th, or D-Day, involved 6,800 vessels, 11,500 aircraft, and 156,000 men. "I hope to God I know what I'm doing," said General Eisenhower, supreme commander of the Allied Expeditionary Force, on the eve of the attack. Given total air superiority, German confusion, brilliant inventions such as the Pluto oil pipeline and artificial "Mulberry" harbors, and also the courage of the English-speaking peoples—of the 4,572 Allied servicemen killed that day, 98.4 percent came from the United States, Britain, Canada, Australia, and New Zealand—victory was assured. Montgomery addressed his troops: "To us is given the honor of striking a blow for freedom which will live in history; and in the better days that lie ahead men will speak with pride of our doings. We have a great and righteous cause."

ABOVE
American craft landing at Omaha Beach on D-Day, June 6, 1940. Heavy casualties were inflicted but by the end of the day they had gained two small footholds on French soil.

OPPOSITE
Some military historians estimate that decryption of German communiqués at Bletchley Park shortened the war by two years.

On December 16, 1944, the Germans launched a major counterattack, driving once again through the wooded mountains of the Ardennes in Belgium. Twenty divisions—seven of them armored—assaulted the American First Army, while to the north SS-Oberstgruppenführer Sepp Dietrich's Sixth Panzer Army struck for the Meuse and General Hasso von Manteuffel's Fifth Panzer Army tried to make for Brussels. Seeing the American front effectively being sliced in half, on December 20th, Eisenhower gave Montgomery command of the whole northern sector; Montgomery's forces successfully engaged the enemy in what has become known as the Battle of the Bulge until December 26th, when the Germans ran out of gasoline and were forced to surrender.

In January 1945, Eisenhower adopted a two-pronged strategy for the invasion of Germany, with the British and Canadian forces pushing down through the Reichswald into the Rhineland from the north, while the Americans came up through the south. The land battle was supported by the heroic missions of Bomber Command and the United States Air Force over such cities as Dresden, Hamburg, Cologne, and Berlin, as well as hundreds of lesser targets. As the diaries of senior Nazis such as propaganda minister Dr. Joseph Goebbels and armaments minister Albert Speer attest, these raids were highly effective in breaking German morale and dislocating industry. But they came at a terribly high cost: during the war as a whole no fewer than 58,000 men died flying missions for Bomber Command.

By mid-March, most of the territory west of the Rhine had been cleared, with the German Army suffering 60,000 casualties and 300,000 being taken prisoner. On April 11th, the American Ninth Army reached the Elbe at Magdeburg, only 80 miles from Berlin, and joined hands with the Red Army. Two weeks later the Russians completed the encirclement of the German capital.

RIGHT
Sachsenhausen concentration camp, 22 miles north of Berlin, was mainly used for political prisoners during the war years. Inmates were forced to produce counterfeit US and British currency in an attempt to destabilize the Allies' economies.

Defeat of the Axis Powers

In January 1945, the Red Army liberated Auschwitz in Poland, where the SS had systematically murdered two million innocent people, 90 percent of them Jews. The true, horrific extent of what the Nazis dubbed "The Final Solution" became apparent over the following months—although it had long been guessed at and more recently known about in ever greater detail—as each extermination camp along the westward route was liberated. In all, the Nazis were found to have killed some six million Jews, along with hundreds of thousands of other innocent political or racial victims of the Third Reich, often using the industrialized method of gassing human beings with the poison Zyklon B in specially constructed chambers.

Hitler committed suicide in his bunker in the Reich Chancellery on April 30, 1945, two days after Mussolini was shot by partisans in northern Italy. Berlin surrendered on May 2nd and, on May 7th, at Eisenhower's headquarters at Reims, General Alfred Jodl and Admiral Hans-Georg von Friedeburg signed the document of total unconditional surrender on behalf of Germany, witnessed by representatives of the United States, Great Britain, France, and Russia. The next day, May 8th, was declared Victory in Europe Day. Churchill sanctioned celebrations, but insisted they should only be short, considering the ongoing conflict with Imperial Japan. In a general election in late July, there was a Labour landslide victory, and Clement Attlee replaced Churchill as prime minister.

It was fortunate, then, that by August 1945, technological science was capable of coming to the service of civilization in the ultimate cause of peace, as two secret projects, codenamed "Tube Alloys" and "Manhattan" respectively, delivered two terrible new weapons, bombs that were capable of using nuclear fission to create explosions of previously unimaginable force. Yet even after one had been dropped on the Japanese city of Hiroshima on August 6th, killing approximately 70,000 people, Japan refused to admit defeat. Only after a second bomb fell on Nagasaki three days later, with the loss of a further 39,000 lives, was Tokyo willing to countenance surrender, so that on August 14, 1945, a conflict that cost the lives of more than 50 million people, was finally brought to an end.

The aftermath of World War II saw profound changes in the map of Europe, the establishment of the United Nations to replace the discredited League of Nations, and the beginning of a Cold War between the capitalist West and the communist Soviet Bloc that would persist until the fall of the Berlin Wall nearly half a century later. Yet for all the terrible sadness and loss, World War II had to be fought, to extirpate the evil of Nazism and to wipe from the earth the satanic figure of Adolf Hitler.

HITLER'S FINAL DAYS

On January 16, 1945, Hitler moved into a bunker in Berlin from which to command his troops as the American and Russian armies approached. On April 22nd, when General Steiner's army failed to materialize to defend Berlin, Hitler knew the war was lost. On April 29th, he married his mistress Eva Braun, ate a wedding breakfast, then dictated his will to his secretary. News arrived that Mussolini's body had been strung up by the heels; he was determined to avoid the same fate, so left instructions for his remains to be burned. On April 30th, he shot himself in the head after Eva Braun had bitten on a cyanide capsule.

BELOW
General Alfred Jodl signs the German surrender in Reims on 7 May 1945, watched by Major Wilhelm Oxenius and Admiral Hans-Georg von Friedeburg.

CHANEL
N°5
COCO
HANS
ARCTIC CIRCLE
JAN MAYEN IS.
ICELAND
FAEROE IS.
SHETLAND IS.
HEBRIDES
NORTH SEA
BALTIC SEA
POLISH S.S.R.
UKRAINIAN S.S.R.
HUNGARIAN S.S.R.
RUMANIAN S.S.R.
CORSICA
SARDINIA
MENORCA
MALLORCA
IBIZA
LISBON
GIBRALTAR
SICILY
GREECE
CRETE
MEDITERRANEAN SEA
BLACK
AZORES ISLANDS
MADEIRA ISLANDS
OUTPOSTS
TROPIC OF CANCER
ALGERIA
LIBYA
EGYPT
SAHARA
WEST AFRICA
TOMBOUCTOU
NIGERIA
SUDAN
KHARTOUM
LIBERIA
CONGO
CABINDA
LAKE VICTORIA
EQUATOR
ASCENSION ISLAND
MARTINIQUE

Coco Chanel & Hans von Dincklage

IDENTITY CARD

HANS GUNTHER VON DINCKLAGE
NAME

GERMAN
NATIONALITY

DECEMBER 15, 1896
DOB

ATTACHÉ AT GERMAN EMBASSY IN PARIS
ROLE

WORKING FOR THE ABWEHR
ORGANIZATION

GABRIELLE "COCO" BONHEUR CHANEL
NAME

FRENCH
NATIONALITY

AUGUST 19, 1883
DOB

ABOVE
Multiple strings of pearls: just one of Coco Chanel's trademark styles.

Tens of thousands of French citizens who had collaborated with the German occupiers were punished after the liberation, but Coco Chanel, who lived with a German spy in Paris throughout the war, somehow managed to escape censure.

Gabrielle "Coco" Chanel was one of the most influential women of the 20th century, with her simple classic designs forever changing the way women dressed. Her love life, on the other hand, was not so successful. There is no doubt that the man she claimed was the great love of her life, Arthur "Boy" Capel, had loved her in return, but as a British man with aristocratic pretensions there was never any chance that he would marry her. Chanel was perceived as working in "trade," had been born out of wedlock, and had spent six years of her childhood in an orphanage after her mother's early death, so she was hardly suitable wife material. She and Boy became lovers in 1910 and remained so even after he married Diana Wyndham, the daughter of Lord Ribblesdale, in 1918. But their trysts were cut short the following year, when Boy was killed in a car accident while driving to join Coco in the South of France, leaving her utterly heartbroken.

BELOW
Coco with Arthur "Boy" Capel on the beach in Saint-Jean-de-Luz, France, 1917: she always said he was the great love of her life.

Coco's next serious affair was with the Duke of Westminster, known to all as Bendor, who was one of the richest men in the world when she began to consort with him in 1924. He was extremely generous, buying her lavish gifts of flowers, jewels, and property. The gossip columns speculated that she would become the third Duchess of Westminster, but by that time Coco was too independent to take on the demanding role of mistress of his family seat and was loath to give up her thriving fashion house. The affair lasted around ten years, even after he remarried in 1930, then faded into friendship.

When Britain and France declared war on Germany on September 3, 1939, Coco was living in an apartment in the Ritz Hotel in Paris, which conveniently backed onto her rue Cambon salon. She decided to close down the House of Chanel and lay off all her staff for the duration of the war, believing that it was no time to be designing glamorous gowns. On June 4, 1940, as German troops approached Paris, she had a chauffeur take her south out of harm's way, but after terms were reached between Hitler and the Vichy government on June 22nd, she decided to come back. She arrived at the Ritz to find it full of German officers. Her apartment had been requisitioned, but the manager

OPPOSITE
Coco and von Dincklage in Villars-sur-Ollon, Switzerland, in 1951. She was almost 13 years his senior.

BELOW
German minister of propaganda Joseph Goebbels emerges from the Ritz Hotel in Paris, July 1940. Many German officers used the hotel as their wartime headquarters.

offered her another room, which she accepted, seeing no reason to give up staying there despite being under the same roof as leading Nazis such as Hermann Göring and Joseph Goebbels.

In September 1940, Chanel noticed a tall, blonde, handsome man in civilian clothes talking to Germany's foreign minister, Joachim von Ribbentrop, in the hotel lobby. She would later claim that she had met him socially several years before, but that they were reintroduced during this period. She asked his advice about a friend of hers who was a prisoner of war. He invited her to dinner and thus began her notorious affair with Baron von Dincklage, known to his friends as "Spatz"– German for "sparrow."

Sleeping with the Enemy

Hans von Dincklage was born in Hanover, son of an English mother and a father who was a baron from Lower Saxony. He was a true aristocrat with a taste for fine food and wine, the best cigars, expensive clothes, and playing polo. He spoke French and English fluently and had impeccable manners, particularly toward women.

His easy charm, good looks, and diplomatic position meant he was invited to mingle in high society.

Spatz enlisted in the army in 1918 and was involved in the investigation into the murders of the socialist revolutionary Rosa Luxembourg and her colleagues after an uprising in January 1919. This brought him to the notice of Admiral Wilhelm Canaris, who subsequently recruited him into the *Abwehr*, the German military intelligence service.

In May 1927, Spatz married Maximiliane Henriette Ida von Schoenebeck, eldest daughter of a Düsseldorf baron, and the following year he was posted to the German embassy in Paris, where he became head of communications. His easy charm, good looks, and diplomatic position meant he was invited to mingle in high society, where he proved popular with the ladies. He divorced Maximiliane in 1935 and later confessed to Coco that since then he had been living with a very wealthy Parisian lady who had had to flee before the Nazis arrived because she was "not 100 percent Aryan."

When they met, Spatz was 43 to Coco's 57 years old, and she must have been flattered when he became her lover. They kept very much to themselves, avoiding the fashionable Paris restaurants and taking holidays at her villa in Roquebrune-Cap-Martin on the Mediterranean coast near Italy. To the few friends who dared to question why she was sleeping with a German, she replied sharply, "He isn't German; his mother was English."

She and Spatz spoke English to each other. They socialized with a small group of her artist, writer, and theater friends, and tried to ignore the ugliness and deprivation around them. He seems to have kept his head down, terrified that the high command might decide to post him on some dangerous mission to Russia or elsewhere on the front line. Both hated the war and yearned for the day when it would be over. And it was this instinct, along with a huge measure of arrogance, that led Coco to suggest to Spatz in the summer of 1943 that perhaps she could help to broker peace between England and Germany. She knew Winston Churchill through her affair with Bendor, as they had often stayed with the Churchills in the South of France. If she could talk to him directly, she felt sure she could persuade him that no more lives need be lost.

A business colleague of Spatz's, Captain Theodor Momm, took her on a trip to Berlin, where she explained her plan to Major Walter Schellenberg, acting chief of intelligence of the *Abwehr*. Straightaway he was interested. Coco would request a meeting with Churchill in Madrid, where she knew the British ambassador Sir Samuel Hoare, and she asked that an old friend, Vera Bate, should accompany her. The Chanel peace mission, known as Operation *Modellhut* ("model's hat"), was on.

Germany on the Run

Chanel's peace plan came to nought, of course, especially after Vera Bate denounced her as a collaborator on arrival at the British embassy in Madrid. She was politely told that Churchill was unable to meet her due to illness, and came back to Paris empty-handed.

Early in 1944, Coco returned to Berlin for a debriefing with Schellenberg. Some biographers claim that she had been recruited into the *Abwehr* and was a paid agent of theirs. Files held by the

COLLABORATORS

Many French citizens assisted the Nazi occupiers, whether through fear or expedience or both. In the arts, anyone who performed for German forces was called a *collabo*. Chanel's friend Serge Lifar became director of ballet at the Opéra and greeted all the top Nazis, including Hitler himself. Edith Piaf frequently sang for German audiences, and Sacha Guitry wrote a book in tribute to Marshal Pétain (considered the greatest collaborator of all) as well as continuing to write and direct for stage and screen. After the liberation, purge committees doled out punishments, with execution the sentence for the most serious cases. Lifar was suspended from the Opéra for a year and Guitry was imprisoned for two months. Piaf got off when it was revealed that she had also worked with the Resistance to help Jews escape. Thousands of women who had affairs with Germans—known as *collaboration horizontale*—were beaten and had their heads shaved. It was a fate Chanel was lucky to avoid.

ABOVE
After the war, Marshal Pétain was found guilty of treason and sentenced to life imprisonment.

BELOW
A collaborator has her head shaved after the liberation of Marseilles.

ABOVE
Walter Schellenberg, intelligence chief and possibly one of Coco's lovers.

French police describe her as agent number F-7124, with the pseudonym "Westminster." It seems more likely that she was being naïve and was sufficiently filled with self-importance to believe she could be an international ambassador working for world peace and would be seen as such, rather than as a traitor working for the Nazis.

In August 1944, as American troops approached Paris, Spatz urged Coco to accompany the retreating German Army so that they could disappear into Switzerland, but she refused to leave France. He warned her she would be in trouble because of her association with him, but she insisted she had done nothing of which to be ashamed. She said a fond farewell to her lover and begged him to keep in touch.

On August 26th, Chanel was on the balcony of a friend's apartment on the rue du Rivoli to watch General de Gaulle and the French Forces of the Interior march from the Arc de Triomphe to the Hôtel de Ville. Millions of French citizens cheered and danced in the street, church bells rang and whistles blew. Two weeks later, Chanel was arrested and taken into custody for questioning about her relationship with von Dincklage. "Is it true you were sleeping with a German?" she was asked.

"A woman my age cannot be expected to look at his passport if she has a chance of a lover."

"Really, sir," she replied, "a woman my age cannot be expected to look at his passport if she has a chance of a lover."

Coco was held in custody for three hours and then released, for reasons that have never been made clear. She wouldn't speak of it afterward, but recent historians have speculated that Churchill himself may have ordered her release because she had incriminating information that he didn't want revealed. The Duke of Windsor—formerly King Edward VIII until his abdication in 1936—and his American wife, Wallis Simpson, had been Nazi sympathizers in the 1930s, and the British government had exiled them to Bermuda for the duration of the war. Churchill approved payments to the Germans in return for them protecting the Duke of Windsor's Paris apartment and his château at Cap d'Antibes. This was in direct contravention of the Trading with the Enemy Act and would have been deeply embarrassing had it become known at the time. Perhaps a telephone call was made, a discreet word was said, and Chanel was set free. Certainly, upon her release she said curtly to her grandniece, "Churchill had me freed."

She could have been targeted by ex-Resistance members in the streets had the story come out, but in a PR masterstroke, Coco announced that she would give free bottles of Chanel No. 5 perfume to the American GIs to take home to their wives and girlfriends, an offer that proved incredibly popular. With the Americans on her side, she was safer in the streets of Paris than she would otherwise have been.

Looking after Spatz

Following the end of hostilities, French public opinion was very much against Coco even after the House of Chanel released a statement saying, "Clearly it wasn't the best period to have a love affair with a German even if Baron von Dincklage was English by his mother and she [Chanel] knew him before the War." Coco staunchly denied all accusations of espionage or working for the Germans, but still decided it was wise to lay low for a while and so did not reopen the House of Chanel until 1954.

With the defeat of Germany, months went by without any word from Spatz, and Coco was consumed with worry about him. When she met an American GI of German heritage named Hans Schillinger, the friend of a photographer with whom Chanel had worked, she gave him $10,000 and asked him to track down her lover and help him to reach his family's estate in Schleswig-Holstein. He was to send her a postcard at the Ritz in Paris when he had any news.

It was not until 1946 that Coco received a postcard from Schillinger telling her that von Dincklage had been held in a prisoner-of-war camp. The American GI had managed to obtain the release of her lover, who had subsequently traveled to Hamburg. He wasn't charged with any

BELOW
The timeless classic perfume, Chanel No. 5, got its name because five was Coco's lucky number.

crimes at the Nuremberg Trials, despite claims from some that he had been a more significant spy than he ever let on to Coco. There was no possibility of getting von Dincklage into France, so she made arrangements for him to be conveyed to Lausanne in Switzerland, where they were finally reunited. His experiences had aged him, but he retained his elegant appearance and charming manners and they resumed their affair, socializing with international royalty at the Beau-Rivages Hotel on the lakefront in Lausanne and at hotels in St. Moritz, Klosters, and Davos.

Coco was recalled to Paris in 1949 to testify at the trial of Baron Louis de Vaufreland, a German agent who had accompanied her on the trip to Madrid, but she staunchly defended him and claimed to the judge that if necessary she could arrange a character reference from people high up in the British government. He was still convicted. Walter Schellenberg, the *Abwehr* intelligence chief, was found guilty at his Nuremberg trial and sentenced to six years' imprisonment. When he died in 1952, Coco paid for his funeral. There were rumors that they had been lovers, but there is no clear evidence of that.

THE NUREMBERG TRIALS

The leaders of Britain, France, the Soviet Union, and America had agreed early in the war that Germans who committed atrocities would be brought to justice, just as they were at the Leipzig Trials after World War I. On November 20, 1945, the International Military Tribunal opened its casebook in the Palace of Justice in Nuremberg and, over the next year, 24 of Hitler's main leaders were brought to trial and 12 were sentenced to death. These included Joachim von Ribbentrop, Martin Bormann and Hermann Göring, all close associates of Hitler, and Hans Frank, who as governor-general of Occupied Poland had been given the nickname, "Slayer of the Poles." The trials were filmed and the newsreel shown in cinemas. For many Germans, this was the first they learned of the atrocities committed in concentration camps. The trials of less senior Nazis continued until 1949, with 142 out of 185 defendants found guilty and 24 sentenced to death.

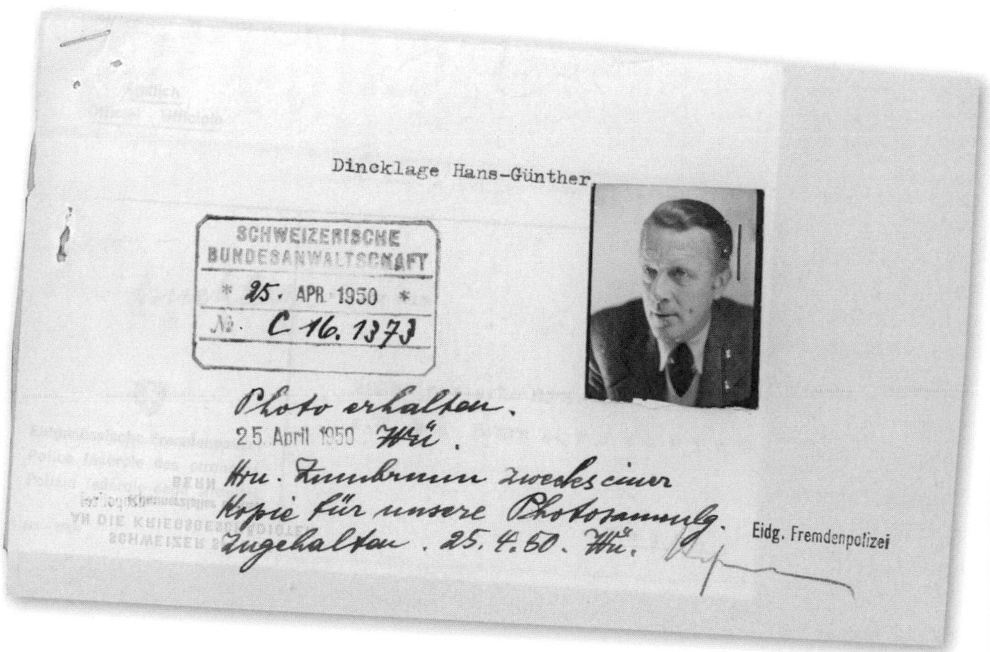
Dincklage Hans-Günther

SCHWEIZERISCHE BUNDESANWALTSCHAFT
* 25. APR 1950 *
№ C 16.1373

Photo erhalten.
25 April 1950 Wü.
Hrn. [illegible] zwecks einer Kopie für unsere Photosammlg.
Zugehalten. 25.4.50. Wü.

Eidg. Fremdenpolizei

ABOVE
Identity papers for Hans von Dincklage in April 1950, around the time his affair with Coco was tailing off.

Questions would continue to be asked about Chanel's relations with the Nazis in wartime, and her biographer and friend Marcel Haedrich said, "If one took seriously the few disclosures that Mademoiselle Chanel allowed herself to make about those black years of the occupation, one's teeth would be set on edge."

Her affair with Spatz seems to have ended around 1950, although she continued to support him for some time afterward—until his next rich lover came along. By then she was well aware, if she hadn't been before, that Spatz was a playboy who let himself be kept in the style to which he was accustomed by wealthy older women. No matter. They had been good company for each other throughout the war and had a genuine affection that transcended politics and nationality. Coco never had another serious love affair.

The relaunch of the House of Chanel fashion line stumbled in France, where Coco was still regarded as a collaborator. The full skirts of Dior's New Look, launched in 1947, made her simple jackets and frocks seem old-fashioned, but she found favor among wealthy British and American clients and released several more successful collections before her death at the age of 87. Spatz continued to live on the goodwill of older women until his own death three years later.

OPPOSITE
The defendants' dock at the Nuremberg court. Nuremberg was thought of as the birthplace of the Nazi Party, so made a fitting location for the trials.

IDENTITY CARD

WILLIAM FAITHFULL ANDERSON
NAME

BRITISH
NATIONALITY

JUNE 17, 1905
DOB

BRIGADIER
ROLE

61 CHEMICAL WARFARE COMPANY, ROYAL ENGINEERS
ORGANIZATION

KATHLEEN HUNT
NAME

BRITISH
NATIONALITY

DECEMBER 19, 1911
DOB

William & Kathleen Anderson

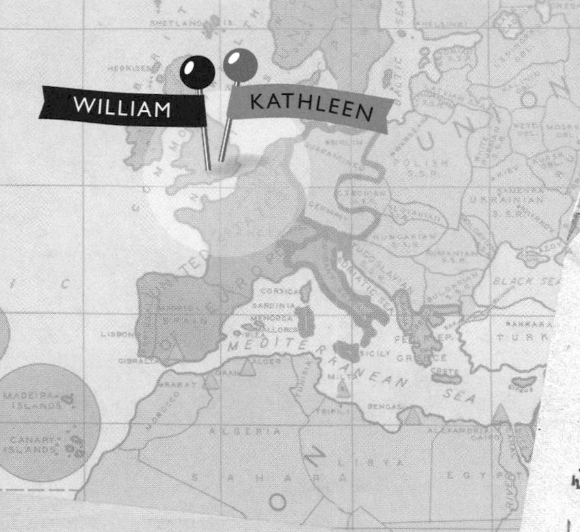

My own darling Kathleen, I warned you
correspondence, didn't I? And I'm sure yo
I'm told letters now get through via Bilbao, s
hearing soon. I think of you and Antony
and of wee Raymond. What incredible ages
in Edinburgh do seem, don't they? I do thank
happy time we had together. The time passes
a settled routine. When
Warringtons; common de
here. He is of course go
but in spite of what som
quite sound. I wish I cou
It is hard for you to pictu
have experts in most lines
officers give first

POST OFFICE TELEGRAM

Prefix. 99 HAND DELIVERY 41 Service Instructions. Words.

99 4:40 LONDON WC OHMS

MRS W F ANDERSON CHENISTON FARNHAM=SURREY =

REGRET TO INFORM YOU THAT MAJOR W F ANDERSON R E HAS BEEN REPORTED BY HIS UNIT AS BELIEVED MISSING FURTHER PARTICULARS WILL BE FORWARDED AS SOON AS RECEIVED =

UNDER SECRETARY OF STATE FOR WAR +

For free repetition of doubtful words telephone "TELEGRAMS ENQUIRY" or call, with this form at office of delivery. Other enquiries should be accompanied by this form and, if possible, the envelope

ABOVE & TOP
Will and Kathleen's wedding at Farnham parish church on August 16, 1938. Members of his company formed a guard of honor.

RIGHT
During their honeymoon, they bicycled around the Isle of Skye.

On May 1, 1940, after eating his breakfast, William Anderson bicycled down the road, waving goodbye to his pregnant wife Kathleen and his one-year-old son, Antony. It would be five years before they saw him again.

Will and Kathleen's mothers were friends long before their children met. The Anderson and Hunt families both moved to Farnham in Surrey around 1930 and began to socialize on a regular basis. Following a commission to the Royal Engineers in 1925, Will had gone to India in 1929 to work as an engineer, building roads and bridges in the mountainous region of the Northwest Frontier. His career path was determined by wherever they chose to send him and thus he was in India throughout the early 1930s, then Egypt in 1936, as part of the force protecting the Western Desert in case Mussolini's troops tried to invade. In 1937, he was in Palestine, then back in India for a while, where his work in building a road through areas rife with tribal tension earned him an MBE and a Military Cross. Later that year, while home in Farnham on leave, he met Kathleen, the daughter of his parents' friends, the Hunts, and it was clear to them both, more or less right away, that they were well matched.

...it was clear to them both, more or less right away, that they were well matched.

The Hunts were a musical family and Kathleen had trained as a cellist at the Royal Academy, where she played under the famous conductor, Sir Henry Wood. Their courtship had to be arranged around his army commitments, so right from the start she had a good idea of the peripatetic lifestyle she could expect when married to such a man. But she was a capable young woman

ABOVE
Their eldest son Antony's christening in Farnham on September 20, 1939.

and ready to set up home with him wherever his career led. They married in August 1938 in Farnham parish church, and during the first year of their married life lived in Manchester, Ireland, and Edinburgh, (where their eldest son was born), then in Winterbourne Gunner in Wiltshire.

When Will left for France with the Royal Engineers on May 1, 1940, Kathleen was in the early weeks of her second pregnancy and wrote in her diary, "Awful day has come. At 8 a.m., after breakfast together, Antony and I said Good-bye to Will." No one knew how long the war would last, and of course she couldn't be sure he would ever come back, but a strong religious faith helped her to cope with this uncertainty. She took Antony back to Farnham to live with her parents, praying every day for Will's safe return.

Captured near Dunkirk

Will's company was sent to the area southeast of Arras in France, near the border with Belgium, where they remained on May 10th when the Germans invaded Holland and Belgium and headed south. In the days that followed, between May 16 and 21, another Panzer division headed north through the Ardennes in Belgium until the British forces realized they were in imminent danger of being encircled and destroyed. A rapid retreat began toward the port of Dunkirk, where on the night of May 26th, the evacuation began. Will's unit was charged with helping to resist the German Seventh Army, and to that end he got his men to push wagons together in a huge locomotive yard to the south of Arras, forming an anti-tank obstacle a mile long and three wagons deep that was extremely useful in holding up the advancing German Army. The unit was then ordered to defend a hill, Mont des Cats, near the Belgian border, before making their way to Dunkirk on foot. But one of Will's men was wounded, slowing their retreat, and just 10 miles short of Dunkirk the party was surrounded and forced to surrender.

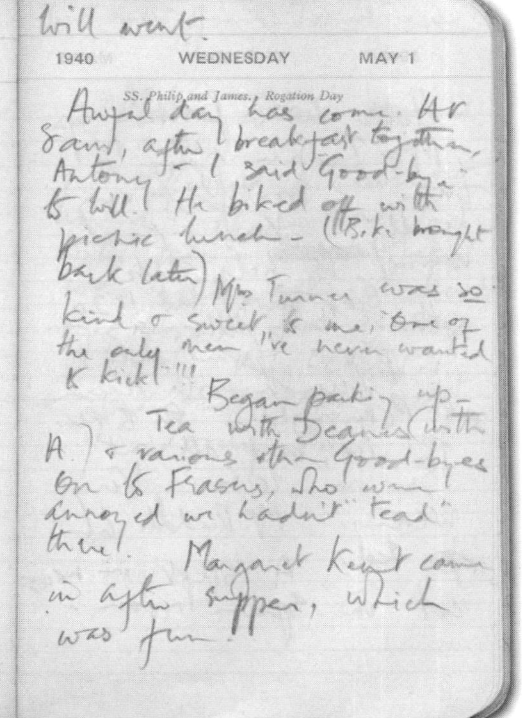
Will went.

1940 WEDNESDAY MAY 1

SS. Philip and James. Rogation Day

Awful day has come. At 8am, after breakfast together, Antony & I said Good-bye to Will! He biked off with picnic lunch – (Bike brought back later) Mr Turner was so kind & sweet to me, One of the only men I've never wanted to kick!!!

Began packing up – Tea with Deanes (with A.) & various other Good-byes. On to Frasers, who were annoyed we hadn't "tead" there! Margaret Kemp came in after supper, which was fun!

BELOW
Kathleen's diary entry for May 1, 1940, the day Will left for France.

Back home, the news from Dunkirk was reported in every news bulletin and Kathleen must have been frantic with worry, hoping against hope that her husband would get onto one of the ships that had sped across the Channel to rescue the troops. But he didn't, and for seven weeks she didn't know whether he was alive or dead. When she finally received a telegram from the War Office telling her that her husband was a prisoner of war (POW) in Laufen Castle on the other side of Germany, it came as something of a relief. At least now he wasn't at risk of dying in battle. Still, she was anxious as her pregnancy advanced. Her worries increased in December when the newborn baby, a boy she named David, developed a condition brought on by stress during pregnancy. Called pyloric stenosis, it caused severe vomiting and required surgery to clear a blockage in the baby's stomach.

In spring 1941, the news came that Will had been part of an attempted escape from Laufen and, as the Germans considered him the ringleader, he was being transferred to Colditz, a castle in Saxony Germany said to be escape-proof. Through the auspices of the Red Cross, Kathleen had begun receiving letters from him.

THE DUNKIRK EVACUATION

Vice-Admiral Bertram Ramsay was charged with organizing the emergency evacuation of Dunkirk during the last week of May 1940. The beaches were very shallow, making it impossible to sail warships right up to the shore, so the call went out to boatyards around the British coast, asking for help. Over 700 "little ships," including fishing boats, yachts, ferries, and pleasure cruisers, joined 220 British Navy warships in their dash across the Channel, so that, in the course of nine days between 27 May and 4 June, the motley fleet managed to rescue an astonishing 192,226 British and 139,997 French soldiers. The beaches were under constant bombardment from the Luftwaffe and 217 craft were sunk, among them 161 of the little ships, but enough of the British Army escaped to allow for a viable fighting force that would soon rise again.

BELOW
Dunkirk, May 1940: soldiers queue to get onto a boat that will take them to safety.

RIGHT
Thinking of home: a photograph of Will taken in Laufen POW camp in late 1940 or early 1941.

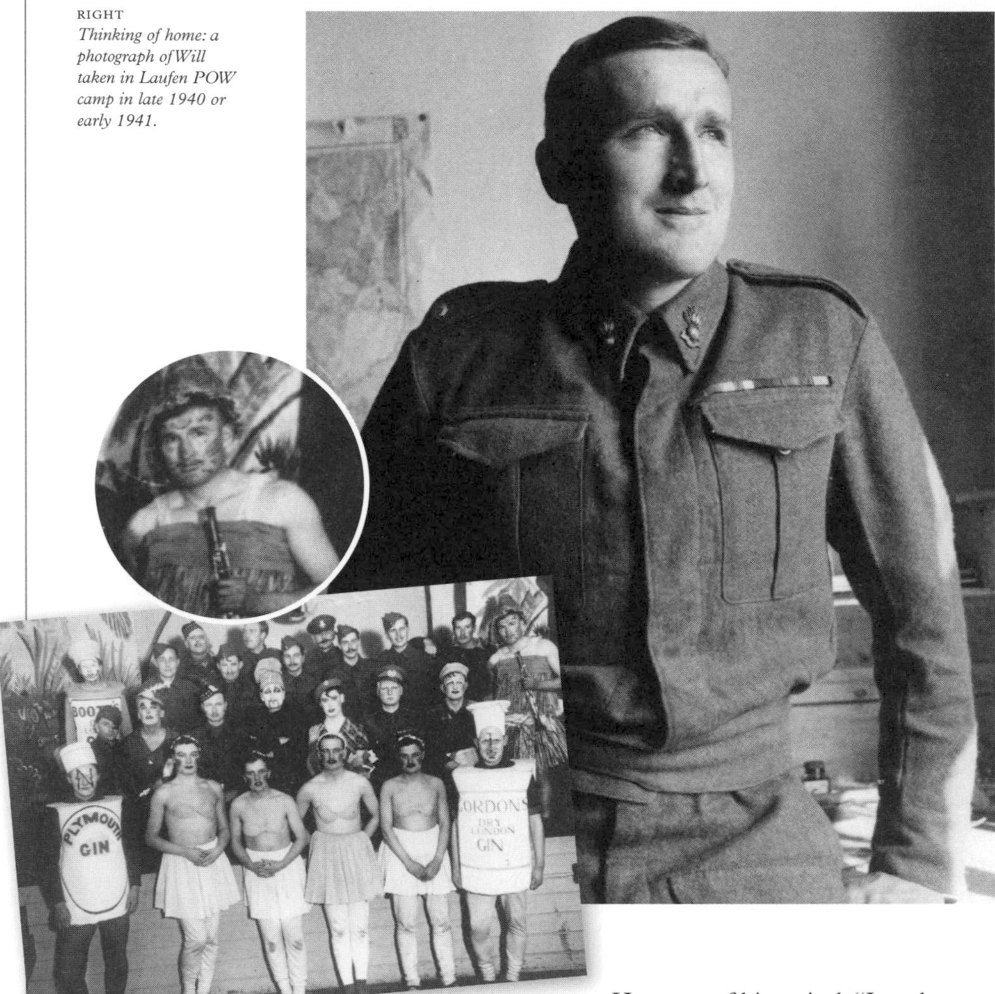

ABOVE
A pantomime the men called "McLaddin" performed at Laufen, with Will as one of the cast (inset above).

He wrote of his arrival: "I got here on Thursday after a journey lasting more than a day. This is rather an interesting camp! We have 200 French and Belgians, 80 Poles and 37 British officers, all a most excellent + enterprising lot." Quite how enterprising they would prove to be, no one could have predicted at the time.

The Spirit of Enterprise

Kathleen and Will weren't a sentimental couple; they were active, practical people who didn't sit around feeling sorry for themselves. In Farnham, Kathleen felt responsible for the families of Will's men who had been captured with him and, because they had a telephone at the house, she helped to share any information received and arrange get-togethers at which the wives could swap news. She also organized a packing center in which Red Cross parcels were prepared before being sent to prisoners of war—only the second such center in the country. Rationing was in force, but Kathleen saved whatever she could in the way of chocolate, butter, cigarettes, and clothing to send to the men, and she urged other POW wives to do the same. She didn't have a lot of money because Will's pay had been cut in half as soon as he was captured, the government assuming that his food and necessities would now be provided by his captors, but Kathleen and the other wives began raising funds in any way they could. She made regular home movies of his sons so that once he returned he would be able to see them at the ages he had missed.

Meanwhile, in Colditz, Will was putting his engineering talents to good use. He became the resident tinsmith, making cooking utensils for the men and helping them to get the maximum amount of food cooked within the limited oven space they were granted. He shared a cell for a while with flying ace Douglas Bader and was escorted by guards down to a blacksmith's shop in Colditz village to help with the repair of Bader's artificial legs. Once an escape

LEFT
David (second from left) and Antony (right) demonstrate their gas masks, along with their cousins. By September 1938, approximately 38 million gas masks had been distributed in Britain in case gas bombs were dropped during air raids.

ABOVE
From left to right, Antony, cousin Robert, and David help to promote fundraising concerts in Farnham.

committee was formed, Will became the person who would create essential items seemingly out of thin air. He constructed a typewriter of sorts and used the Gothic handwriting he had learned at school to forge false identity papers for escapees. When they needed a camera to take photographs for those papers, he made one out of some old spectacles and a few bits of wood. And in the final days of the war, he helped some men who were building a glider in the attic by constructing a false wall to hide it from the Germans and an invisible trapdoor to allow access from below.

Will supported a number of escape attempts—on D-Day he was in solitary confinement after having been caught digging a tunnel under the dentist's chair—but he didn't try to escape himself, considering it "a young man's game." He was in his late thirties, while the men who escaped were mostly in their early twenties. As well as helping with escape attempts, he spent his time playing the oboe in the prison orchestra and painting watercolors of the camp and its surroundings. He was even allowed to send his paintings to Kathleen, and it was from one of these that she learned with delight that he had received a photo she'd sent of his sons, as she could see it painted into the view of his cell.

> *...on D-Day he was in solitary confinement after having been caught digging a tunnel...*

Back in Farnham, Kathleen organized exhibitions of prisoners' art and also played at fundraising concerts. Her young sons paraded the streets wearing sandwich boards to promote forthcoming events, and her POW packing center grew and grew. Keeping busy must have helped—that and waiting for the two letters and two postcards a month that Will was allowed to send. There was only room for 20 lines in each and they were heavily censored. Will devised a secret code while in Laufen, sending her a clue in one letter that it took her six months to figure out—he was asking her to send maps of Yugoslavia. She forwarded the request to the intelligence service MI9, who agreed to take care of it. In fact, the POW wives preferred that their men didn't try to escape, as they wanted them back alive.

The End in Sight

After 76 men escaped from Stalag Luft III camp in March 1944, Hitler was incensed and ordered that anyone escaping should be shot, and after D-Day in June 1944, conditions became harsher at Colditz. Rations were cut, fuel was in short supply, and there were no more food parcels from home. By early 1945, as the US Army advanced from the west and the Russians approached from the east, the situation had become especially volatile. It was feared that the German SS might decide to make a last stand in Colditz Castle and shoot all the prisoners to keep them from interfering. Alternatively, they worried that the Americans and Russians might shell Colditz, suspecting Germans to be holed up in there. Against this backdrop, the men worked hard on their glider, making its wings from bedsheets coated in boiled millet starch, wrapped around a wooden frame. If necessary, it was hoped two men could escape in that aircraft and somehow raise the alarm.

In the final days of the war, however, the camp commandant was persuaded to turn over the interior of the castle to the men and on April 16th, the US First Army arrived to liberate Colditz. Will was going home after five years' absence. One of the last things he did before leaving Colditz was to take a Red Cross food parcel to the blacksmiths in the village. "I never had any problem with ordinary Germans, who were in the same boat as we were," he later explained.

On the day they expected him back in Farnham, Will's young sons planted Union Jacks in their sandpit in the driveway, but their father didn't appear, having been delayed during the journey and his obligatory debriefing by the military authorities. At last Kathleen persuaded the boys

BELOW
This letter Will wrote from Laufen contained a coded message: "I am in a camp in Laufen Bavaria. I hope to be able to escape later on. Maps of Yugoslavia and Hungary would be useful."

27 June 1940.

My own darling Kathleen, I long to hear from you but expect nothing for another month. Remember what I said at the end of last letter about irregularity. Dont you worry about me! I am in a good camp, in with a Large and sufficiently bright and varied assortment of fellows. I hope to be able to describe a person or two later on. Many details impossible of course. Dont you go over-doing it or slaving away to save money. Dont go hungry of rationed food to send here; anything easily got would be useful. I understand all containers will be kept by the authorities, so a good proportion of things like dates, chocolate, raisins and biscuits would be use-ful, but other tinned stuff we can open and eat at once as a mess, or put in fresh containers. Please send a pair of warm pyjamas and my old Burberry raincoat with crowns on the shoulders to make it wearable as uniform, also a good big housewife! also A pair old breeches, khaki shorts and shirt, old brown shoes and gymn. shoes and stockings. Time goes fast here, teaching German and learning other things – it is almost like a University. God keep you and Antony safe my darling. My love to all. It will all come right. From your own Will.

ESCAPE ATTEMPTS FROM COLDITZ

More than 20 tunnels were dug from Colditz Castle during the war, of which the longest one was dug from the wine cellar by the French over the course of nine months. The plan was for 200 prisoners to escape in one night, but in January 1942 the tunnel was discovered when less than seven feet short of completion. In another attempt, one very short man escaped in a Red Cross tea chest, while in another a man was sewn into an old mattress. Two Polish lieutenants tried to climb down a 118-foot wall using a rope made of bed sheets. Men disguised themselves as German officers, in one case as the camp electrician, and even as women. However, once they got out, they still had to make their way to the safety of a neutral country and most were recaptured. Estimates of the number of "home runs" (i.e., prisoners who made it all the way home) vary between 30 and 36. Airey Neave, who went on to become a politician in Margaret Thatcher's shadow cabinet before being killed by an IRA car bomb in 1979, was one of the British officers who made it back safely.

to go to bed, and in the morning they woke up to find a man sitting at their breakfast table that Antony couldn't remember and David had never met.

In one of his letters, Will had promised that on his return he would give the boys presents as if it were an extra birthday. As good as his word, he made some waddling wooden ducks which, he told them, walked the same way as his old cellmate Douglas Bader. That summer the family went to the Isle of Wight on vacation, and Will spent many happy days digging in the sand in the open air, building castles and dams for his children—just the therapy needed after years of fruitless tunneling in Colditz!

It must have been difficult for Will and Kathleen to readjust to married life after so long apart, but they came from a generation that didn't expect marriage to be one long bed of roses. Soon they were on the move again, as later in 1945 Will was sent back to Germany to translate documents for war crimes trials and 1947 found them in India at the time of the Delhi riots following Partition. Kathleen threw herself into delivering babies in a makeshift camp in which some 40,000 Muslim refugees, who had flooded across the new border, were living in horrific conditions. Next, the family (which had expanded to include another boy, Stuart, and a girl, Margaret) was sent to Tanganyika (now Tanzania) in East Africa, where Will helped organize the building of a church, before they were off again to Malaysia in 1953. Throughout their travels, Will continued to sketch and paint, Kathleen played music and taught cello, and together they were able to enjoy a richly creative marriage.

It was a strange start to married life, having such a short time together as husband and wife before being separated for five long years, but Will and Kathleen were both determined, family-centered people who gave their all to whatever they were doing and who complemented one another perfectly.

OPPOSITE
Colditz: the Castle complex within the town of Colditz, near Leipzig.

BELOW
Colditz, winter 1941: Will (left) with his friend Captain M. van der Heyvel of the Royal Netherlands Indies Army. They were known as "Andy and Vandy."

BILL
NORMA
HUDSON BAY
LABRADOR
QUEBEC
ONTARIO
MANITOBA
ALBERTA
COLUMBIA
MONTANA
WYOMING
NEVADA
UTAH
COLORADO
ARIZONA
TEXAS
GULF OF MEXICO
MEXICO
WEST INDIES
CARIBBEAN SEA
VENEZUELA
COLOMBIA
ECUADOR
GUIANA
BRAZIL
PERU
BOLIVIA
SECURITY OUTPOSTS
TROPIC OF CANCER
EQUATOR
AZORES ISLANDS
MADEIRA ISLANDS
CANARY ISLANDS
CAPE VERDE ISLANDS
BERMUDA
GALAPAGOS ISLANDS (ECUADOR)
NEWFOUNDLAND
HUDSON STRAIT
DAVIS STRAIT
DENMARK STRAIT

Bill & Norma Kay Moore

IDENTITY CARD

WILLARD "BILL" MOORE
NAME

AMERICAN
NATIONALITY

DECEMBER 27, 1923
DOB

STAFF SERGEANT
ROLE

3438TH QUARTERMASTER CORPS
ORGANIZATION

NORMA KATHERINE "KAY" DEFREESE
NAME

AMERICAN
NATIONALITY

MARCH 2, 1923
DOB

PRIVATE FIRST CLASS
ROLE

WOMEN'S ARMY CORPS
ORGANIZATION

BACKGROUND
Bill wanted to be a farmer, but these dreams were put on hold when he was drafted into the Army in 1943.

BELOW
Norma wasn't looking for romance when she volunteered. She hoped to travel and see more of the world.

All the girls liked Bill Moore, but when he cheekily asked Norma for a date while he was on the way to meet another girl, at first she refused. Fortunately, he was a very persuasive man who wouldn't take "No" for an answer...

Both Bill and Norma came from big families: he was the tenth of 14 children who grew up in Tuskegee, Alabama; she was the ninth of 11 from Hillburn, New York, brought up by a single mother after her father died at an early age. On leaving high school, Bill worked as a barber in order to pay for his training as a mechanic and farmer at the Tuskegee Institute. One semester he was taught by the renowned scientist George Washington Carver, who designed methods with which poor southern farmers could grow crops in soil that had been depleted by decades of cotton-growing. Farming was what Bill most wanted to do, but he was drafted into the Army in October 1943 and assigned to truck driving on account of his mechanical skills.

BELOW
An all-black regiment, the 41st Engineers, perform a flag ceremony, June 1942.

Norma was at a cousin's birthday party on December 7, 1941, when the music playing on the radio was interrupted by an announcer telling them the grave news that Japan had attacked Pearl Harbor. War was officially declared by Franklin D. Roosevelt the next day. In a burst of patriotism, some of Norma's brothers immediately enlisted, and she decided she too wanted to do her part. "I loved my country," she would tell her family later in life. "I signed on to serve my country and to see the world, and to send home money to Mama, who really needed it badly." Norma had clerical and secretarial training, so after signing up for the Women's Army Corps (WAC) she was sent to Fort Jackson,

"I signed on to serve my country and to see the world."

South Carolina, to do clerical work for the Army's medical departments. She was keen to be sent to Europe, but for the early years of the war she was considered more useful in South Carolina.

On Easter Sunday 1944, Norma was sitting on the grass outside her barracks reading a book of poetry when Bill came by. "All I could see then was the prettiest girl in the world sitting by herself," he would later recall. He was on his way to a date with another girl in Norma's barracks, but he stopped dead in his tracks and began chatting to Norma, then asked if he could take her out. She rebuked him that it wasn't right to have a date with one girl then ask another out, but he was a talkative, persuasive man and he just kept on asking until she gave in. "I do not know why," she would say. "Ordinarily I would have scolded him."

They had a few dates and found they both liked walking in the countryside and had a love of nature. After walks they went for an ice cream soda at the soda fountain shop on the base and all the time they talked about their lives. "I did not join the army to meet a man," Norma used to say, adding that she knew a lot of the other girls did. But this one was very romantic and she soon found herself being swept off her feet.

It was "probably the craziest thing I ever did," she would say with a chuckle.

Bill knew that he would soon be sent to Europe and he also knew that he couldn't risk letting this very special girl slip through his fingers, so two weeks after meeting Norma he asked her to marry him. She was normally a reserved, cautious person but found herself saying "Yes." It was "probably the craziest thing I ever did," she would say with a chuckle. On June 12th, they tied the knot in a small chapel wedding in South Carolina, with her brother Stanley the only family member able to attend. They had a few days' honeymoon on the South Carolina shore and then he was shipped out to England. They said goodbye with absolutely no idea when—or if—they would ever see each other again.

Driving the Red Ball Express

After the D-Day landings in Europe, as Allied combat troops pushed forward through France, there was an urgent need for supply convoys to get food, ammunition, artillery, medical supplies, and gasoline to the front line. The French railway system

RACIAL SEGREGATION IN WARTIME

In 1939, fewer than 4,000 African-Americans were serving in the US forces and only 12 of them were officers. The Army was strictly segregated, with African Americans in all-black units, while the Air Corps simply didn't accept African-American pilots until October 1940 and the Marine Corps excluded them for most of the war. Even so, more than a million African-Americans joined up during the war and made a significant contribution to the war effort, although many were confined to subordinate roles such as cooks, janitors, and waiters. There was racial integration in the British Commonwealth forces, but the American commanders still believed that "mixing of the races" would lead to trouble. Famous African-American units such as the Tuskegee Airmen, the 761st Tank Battalion, and the 452nd Anti-Aircraft Artillery Battalion performed with such bravery, as did units like Bill Moore's working alongside white units, that they helped pave the way for President Truman's order, signed in 1948, to desegregate the troops.

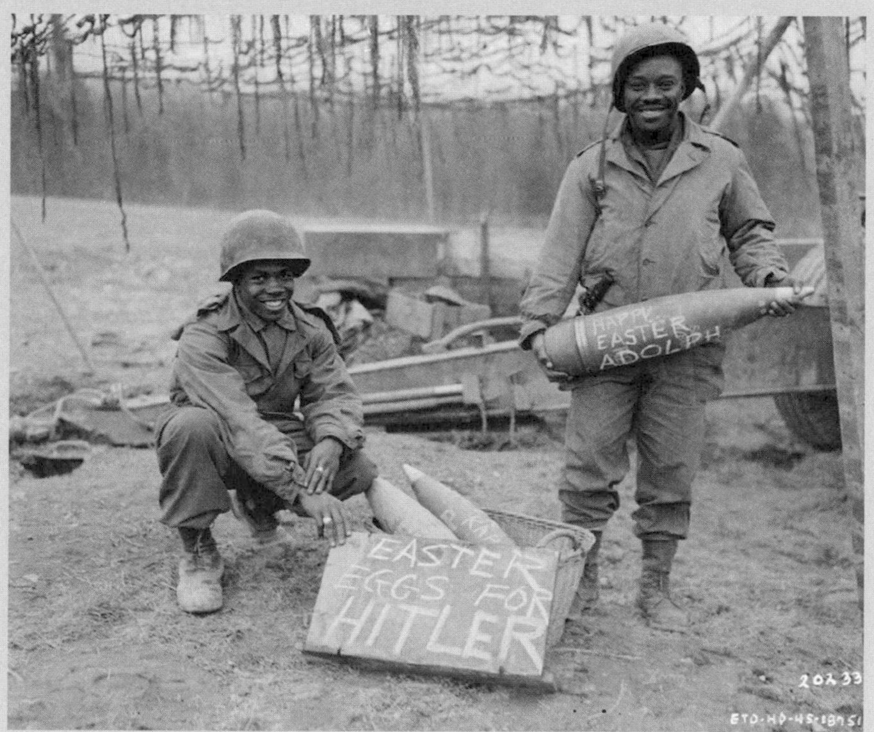

ABOVE
March 10, 1945: William E. Thomas and Joseph Jackson display their "Easter eggs for Hitler" (actually 155mm artillery shells) shortly before firing them.

had been destroyed by Allied bombing raids and by Resistance sabotage in the weeks before D-Day to prevent the German Army from reaching the Normandy coast, so trains could not be used. Instead, a huge truck convoy system, called the Red Ball Express, was created. Three-quarters of the truck drivers were African-American, and Bill Moore was one of them.

The first Red Ball Express set off on August 25, 1944. Three thousand trucks drove in convoys, 60 yards apart, and speed limiters in the engines meant they all traveled at exactly 25 mph. "I remember thinking we must look like a row of ducks," Bill used to say. German planes swooped overhead and fired at them, but fortunately he wasn't hurt. They were constantly on the lookout for enemy aircraft, landmines, and potential ambushes, making it a hair-raising experience, but they reached the front line, unloaded their cargo, and on the return trip were given the solemn duty of carrying back the coffins of American soldiers who had been killed.

BELOW
Drivers of the 666th Quartermaster Truck Company covered at least 20,000 miles each across Holland, France, and Central Europe.

After that first convoy, Bill and his friends disobeyed direct orders by taking the speed limiters off their trucks so that they would have more flexibility under attack and, equally importantly, so that they could finish their runs as quickly as possible. At night they had to drive with tape over their headlights, reducing them to narrow cat's-eye slits, making the runs even more nerve-racking. But Bill did at least have a machine gun on board and on one occasion tried to shoot down a German plane, though without success.

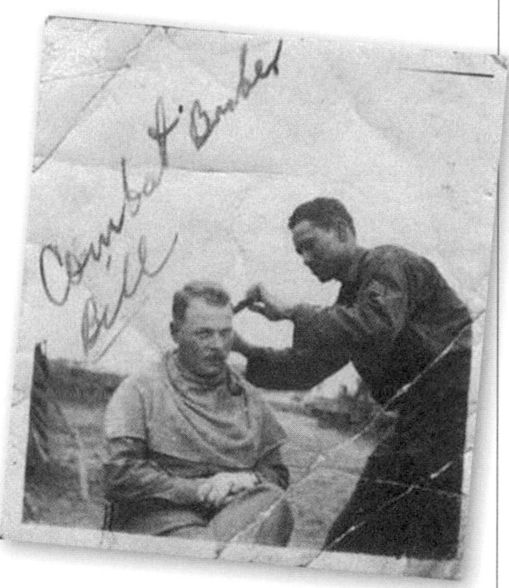

ABOVE
Combat Barber Bill: it was through chatting with an officer whose hair he was trimming that Bill learned Norma was going to be in Rouen in June 1945.

Back at base between missions, Bill was much in demand for his hair-cutting skills, and he enjoyed the camaraderie with the men and the healthy competition between Red Ball drivers. According to him, African-Americans were much better drivers and white guys "would grind gears like coffee." He wrote regular letters to Norma and she wrote to him, but it was hard not being able to see the wonderful woman he had known for only three short months before he came to Europe.

By November 1944, the Red Ball Express was no longer needed, because railway lines had been repaired and gas pipelines installed in sufficient quantity. Supplies could also now be brought in through the Belgian ports. Bill was still driving a truck, but now his responsibilities included collecting Americans who had been held in prisoner-of-war camps and transporting German soldiers who had surrendered. And as spring arrived, he was handed an altogether more harrowing job.

On April 4, 1945, Bill was part of the Army that liberated the Buchenwald concentration camp. A little Jewish man "who looked like a dead man walking" staggered up to Bill, called him "'an American,'' then fell into his arms and hugged him "like nobody ever hugged me in my life." It was desperately moving for Bill on many different levels: he looked at these people, most of them half-dead, and wondered how God could let men do this to each other; and he also realized it was the first time anyone had ever called him an American and that it was "like I was as good as any American he was like to find." Back home, he was called many things but none of them were "American."

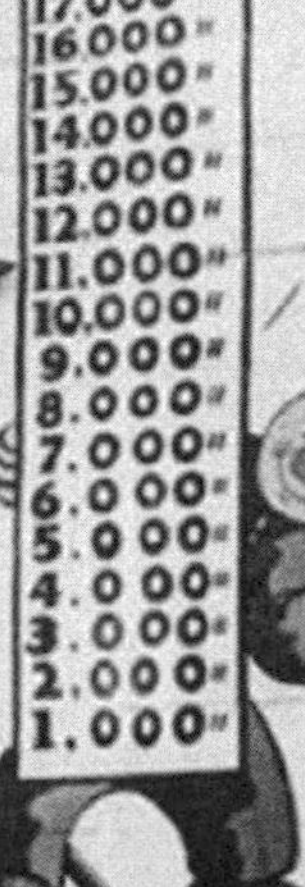
To-days
TONNAGE
TARGET
20.000 TONS
19.000
18000
17.000
16.000
15.000
14.000
13.000
12.000
11.000
10.000
9.000
8.000
7.000
6.000
5.000
4.000
3.000
2.000
1.000
RED BALL
HIGHWAY
STAY ON THE
KEEP 'EM
ROLLING!

BALL

RED BALL ACHIEVEMENTS

By mid-August, the American First and Third Armies had advanced so far across France that they had become separated from their supply teams and had to stop due to what General Patton called a critical shortage of "beans, bullets, and gas." The commanders sat down to brainstorm a solution and the Red Ball Express was devised. Two Red Ball routes would run from Cherbourg, where the trucks were loaded, to a forward base at Chartres, southwest of Paris: the northern route was for supplies going out to the troops and the southern one was for the return journey. At its height, there were 5,958 trucks carrying about 20,000 tons of supplies a day on journeys of around 400 miles for a round trip. The name "Red Ball" came from a railroad term for goods designated "perishable"and requiring shipment as a priority, and the sides of the trucks and signposts along the routes had a characteristic red ball painted on them indicating that they should be given priority over civilian traffic. During the three months it was in operation, the Red Ball Express broke all previous records for supply of goods to the military. As Colonel John S. D. Eisenhower, son of the Allied supreme commander, later put it when recalling the events of the time, "Without Red Ball the advance across Europe could not have been made."

As well as Buchenwald, Bill was involved in the liberation of prisoners from Dora-Mittelbau on April 10th and Mauthausen on May 5th and, throughout that period, he helped to transport survivors of Birkenau, part of the Auschwitz complex. He saw some shocking sights that would remain with him for the rest of his days.

A Surprise Reunion

After Bill left for Europe, Norma was eager to go there as well, but the Army was still strictly segregated, so there weren't many units she could join. Eventually, in the winter of 1944–45, she was assigned to the 6888th Central Postal Directory Battalion based in Birmingham, England, a unit consisting of 855 African-American women and led by Major Charity Adams Early, the highest-ranking African-American woman in the war. Their role was crucial for the morale of the troops, because they helped to make sure that letters reached the correct recipients—a mammoth task, since at this stage there were some seven million Americans in Europe whose constant movements brought about an estimated 30,000 changes

OPPOSITE
A military policeman directs traffic on a Red Ball route. Approximately three-quarters of Red Ball drivers were African-American.

of address per day. All were waiting for mail from their families and friends at home, and the women of the 6888th worked three shifts, seven days a week, to try and get it delivered in good time.

They got along well with the local people in Birmingham and the *Birmingham Sunday Mercury* noted: "These WACs are very different from the coloured women portrayed in films … [they] have dignity and proper reserve." In the spring of 1945, they were sent to Paris and Norma was astonished and delighted that wherever they went people offered to buy drinks for them, so grateful were they for the liberation of their country. It was quite different from the treatment she was used to at home in Hillburn, where the schools and public amenities were racially segregated.

In June 1945, as her first wedding anniversary approached, Norma was based in Rouen. Bill discovered her location from an officer whose hair he was cutting and determined that he would see his bride on their anniversary. He would never have been approved for leave, so on June 12th he went AWOL, borrowing jeeps, trucks, and motorcycles to make an epic journey

BELOW
Norma was delighted to be able to visit Shakespeare's birthplace in Stratford-upon-Avon while stationed in Birmingham.

BOTTOM
While in Rouen, members of the 6888th marched across the town square in memory of Joan of Arc, who was burned at the stake there on May 30, 1431.

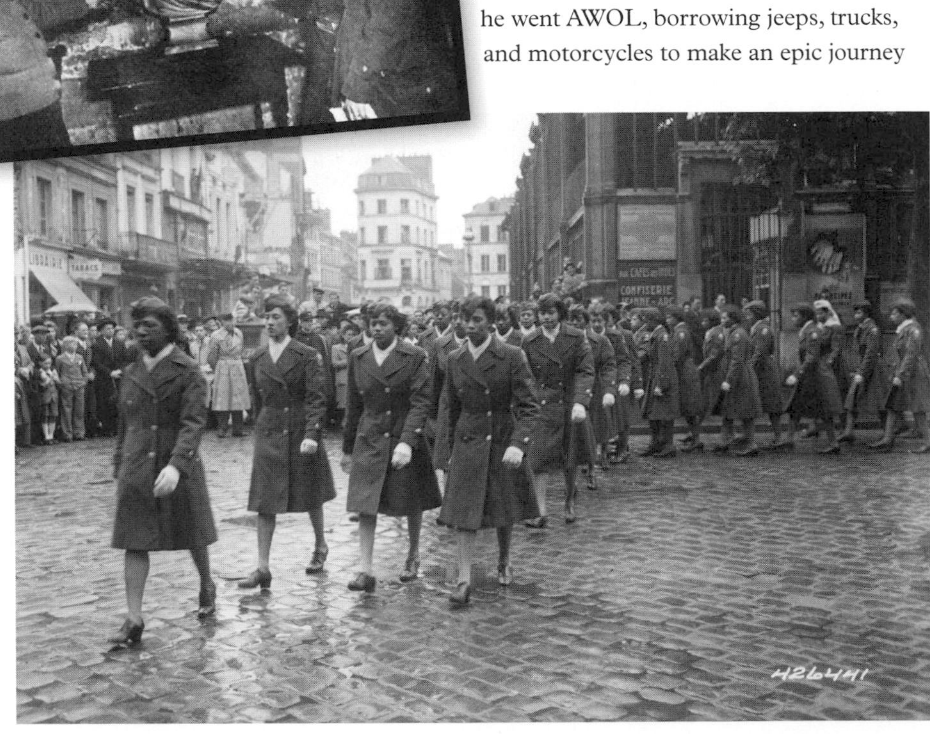

across France from Germany. He messaged Norma's captain that he was coming, asking her to keep it a secret.

...they loved each other with a fierce passion from those early days back in Fort Jackson...

Unsuspecting, Norma was sitting in a cafe with a girlfriend when in walked her grinning husband. It was the first time they had seen each other in almost a year. "Well, we just hugged and kissed," she recalled. He'd brought her a tin of semi-sweet Swiss chocolate as an anniversary present, and she said that, though it was the most delicious thing she had ever tasted, seeing him was the best gift of all. He couldn't stay long without risking court martial, so he turned around and drove all the way back within 24 hours. He got along so well with his commanding officers that he escaped punishment for the exploit; his wife, of course, would never forget the romantic gesture he made that day.

"After all the war and ugliness, I had to see the person I loved the most," he explained. Norma helped to remind him of the good things in life at a time when he was seeing too many of the bad.

Making a Life Back Home

Norma was the first to return to the United States, in September 1945, with Bill following in November. They were joyfully reunited at her mother's home in Hillburn, where the rest of her family were able to meet Bill for the first time. They traveled south to Tuskegee for him to finish his training, but were back in Hillburn for the birth of their first child, Nancy. Bill got a job as a mechanic, servicing and repairing trucks, and he continued to work as a self-employed barber. In 1960, he became one of the first black members of the New York State chapter of the International Union of Operating Engineers, and he earned a good salary, but an accident at work in the early 1970s caused severe burns to his hands and forced him to take early retirement. By that time Bill and Norma were proud to own a lovely three-bedroom house with ten acres of land in a town called Pine Bush, where their four children went through school alongside the children of their white neighbors.

Bill and Norma were quite different characters—he was always the more gregarious of the two—but they loved each other with a fierce passion from those early days back in Fort Jackson right through to the end of their lives.

IDENTITY CARD
DESMOND PAUL HENRY
NAME
BRITISH
NATIONALITY
JULY 5, 1921
DOB
TECHNICAL CLERK AND STAFF SERGEANT
ROLE
R.E.M.E (ROYAL ELECTRICAL AND MECHANICAL ENGINEERS)
ORGANIZATION
MARRIED MAY 19, 1945
LOVE STORIES
LOUISA HENRIETTE JEANETTE BAYEN
NAME
BELGIAN
NATIONALITY
MAY 1, 1920
DOB
WORLD WAR II
MARRIED MAY 19, 1945
LOVE STORIES
GREENLAND
JONES SOUND
BEAUFORT
EQUATOR
PEACE-SECURITY
PAUL

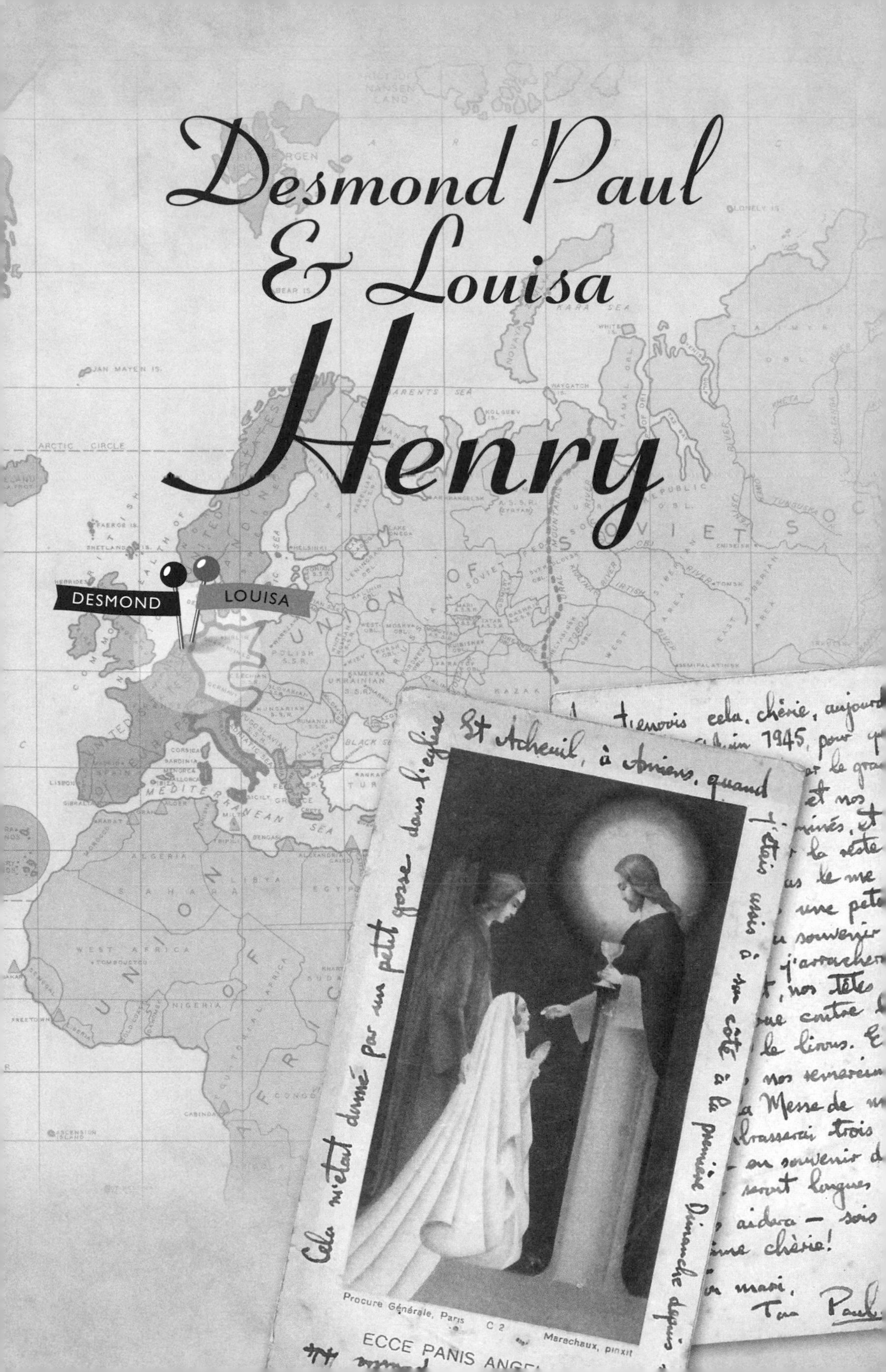

Desmond Paul & Louisa Henry

DESMOND

LOUISA

TOP
With the boys in France, 1944. Desmond, sporting a moustache, is on the left side of the front row.

RIGHT
Photograph of Louisa, with the inscription, "Paul, mon amour, de tout mon coeur, Loup'" (Paul, my love, with all my heart, Loup).

War disrupted Desmond and Louisa's plans for the future, but far from ruining their lives, it enabled them to improve their prospects and achieve a better standard of living than they might have otherwise—not least because it brought them together.

From an early age, it was obvious that Desmond was an unusual boy: he preferred reading encyclopedias to playing football and spent hours poring over the boiler parts catalogs his father brought home from work. His hero was Leonardo da Vinci, and Desmond also aspired to be an artist and an inventor, spending his pocket money on drawing paper upon which he avidly sketched. So strong was his urge to draw that his parents even let him daub his bedroom walls! As devout Catholics, Desmond's parents had to petition to get him into Huddersfield College, a Church of England establishment in Yorkshire, but the only locally available grammar school. Once there, he shone academically and also acquired a reputation for pulling stunts: a particular favorite was placing a paper bag filled with homemade flashpowder on the tramlines, which created a mini explosion when crushed by tram wheels; this caused the tram to brake suddenly and greatly puzzled the tram driver, who would leap out of his cab to look under the vehicle only to find nothing there. Desmond passed all his school subjects—including French—with flying colors, but unfortunately the family couldn't raise the money for him to study A levels and go to university, so at the age of 16 he sat the council exam to become a junior clerk in the offices of Huddersfield Waterworks.

Desmond passed all his school subjects—including French—with flying colors

By contrast, Louisa's childhood in Liège, Belgium, was overshadowed by tragedy. Her father, who had been a miner for 34 years, since the age of ten, died of pneumonia. Louisa was just two years old, but she never forgot watching her grief-stricken mother wrap his feet in scarves, trying desperately to keep her father warm as the coldness of death gradually took hold. For the next five years, Louisa was dressed only in black mourning clothes, and they

ABOVE
Desmond (front row, second from left) with some of his comrades from the Royal Electrical and Mechanical Engineers, which was formed in October 1942 to maintain all the army's electrical and mechanical equipment.

struggled to survive on the money her mother made as a cleaning woman and seamstress. She worked such long hours that Louisa was what we would now call a "latchkey kid," letting herself in after school and waiting alone until her mother came home at around eight in the evening. Louisa nevertheless did very well at school and, at the age of 14, she won a place to train as a primary school teacher at the prestigious École Normale in Liège, where the teachers encouraged her and discreetly loaned her the money to buy textbooks. She knew it would be difficult for her to marry someone from an educated background, since at that time in Belgium, girls required a dowry in order to marry well and there was simply no one to provide one for her. Then in May 1940, just as Louisa was celebrating her 20th birthday and graduating as a primary school teacher, Hitler's troops swept into the country and everything changed overnight.

A Fateful Meeting

Desmond volunteered for the Territorial Army in September 1938, when he and his family believed war was imminent; in this way, in the event of war he couldn't be conscripted as "cannon fodder." He chose to become a technical clerk with the Royal Electrical and Mechanical Engineers, which would let him pursue his interests in machinery and technology. He was sent to a base near Cardiff, Wales, where he ran the office that ordered spare parts for anti-aircraft guns and sometimes helped out in the workshops mending equipment. He also took advantage of a scheme whereby military personnel had free access to art history classes at Cardiff Art Gallery. On Saturday nights, the soldiers all went to the local dance and Henry met one girl he liked enough to give her his rosary beads, but nothing more came of it.

Louisa was unable to find a job as a primary school teacher in Liège and risked being rounded up to work in a German labor camp if she remained unemployed. She asked around, and through one of the women for whom her mother provided sewing services, they were both offered jobs and accommodation in Brussels, working for a Belgian woman who had a jewelry business. Louisa would be a secretary while her mother would be a cleaning woman, and they could live in a flat above the premises at 19 Rue du Pont Neuf. It was a colorful area of central Brussels, with a brothel-cum-transvestite cafe on the same street, but they were relieved to be "safe" given the horror stories they heard of what was happening to those around them in Occupied Belgium.

In 1942, a young woman called Elly Gelenne came to hide in the house, distraught because her husband Paul, who worked for a Resistance group, had just been arrested by the Gestapo. Louisa and her mother comforted Elly as she awaited news and then consoled her when, in March 1943, she read in the local paper that Paul had been executed. Life was tough in many ways: the rations for a month only lasted a week, after which they were forced to buy essentials on the black market, and there was no money for new clothes, so they had to use their sewing skills to "make do and mend." Louisa was a sociable girl who liked meeting people but she spent most evenings at home with her mother and Elly, hoping and praying for the day when the Occupation would finally end.

For the first years of the war, Desmond was based in England, but in June 1944 he was sent to France as part of the support team behind the second wave of the Normandy landings. The realities of war quickly came home to him when the troopship on which he was to be transported across the Channel was bombed as it lay moored in port. It was hit by what turned out to be a

BELOW
Desmond arrived at Le Hamel, Normandy, in June 1944. Tanks and motor vehicles were driven directly onto the beach.

D-DAY

The Allied invasion of Normandy began on the evening of June 5, 1944, when two groups of Allied bombers dropped tinfoil strips over Pas-de-Calais to confuse German radar, then just after midnight on June 6th, 1,760 tons of bombs were dropped on German troops defending the Normandy coast. A total of 6,500 vessels crossed the Channel carrying 194,000 troops to five beaches codenamed Sword (British troops), Juno (Canadian), Gold (British), Omaha (US), and Utah (US). By the end of the day, 150,000 men were ashore and the only German division in the area had been scattered. It would take six more weeks of fierce fighting before they were able to advance out of Normandy, but a foothold in Occupied Europe had been established after one of the most remarkable pieces of military planning the world had ever seen.

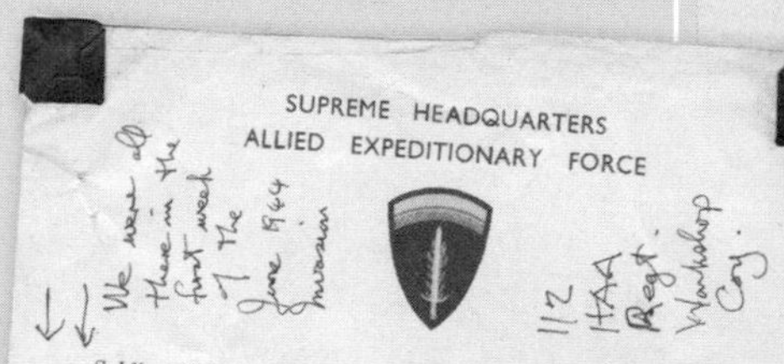

SUPREME HEADQUARTERS
ALLIED EXPEDITIONARY FORCE

Soldiers, Sailors and Airmen of the Allied Expeditionary Force!

You are about to embark upon the Great Crusade, toward which we have striven these many months. The eyes of the world are upon you. The hopes and prayers of liberty-loving people everywhere march with you. In company with our brave Allies and brothers-in-arms on other Fronts, you will bring about the destruction of the German war machine, the elimination of Nazi tyranny over the oppressed peoples of Europe, and security for ourselves in a free world.

Your task will not be an easy one. Your enemy is well trained, well equipped and battle-hardened. He will fight savagely.

But this is the year 1944! Much has happened since the Nazi triumphs of 1940-41. The United Nations have inflicted upon the Germans great defeats, in open battle, man-to-man. Our air offensive has seriously reduced their strength in the air and their capacity to wage war on the ground. Our Home Fronts have given us an overwhelming superiority in weapons and munitions of war, and placed at our disposal great reserves of trained fighting men. The tide has turned! The free men of the world are marching together to Victory!

I have full confidence in your courage, devotion to duty and skill in battle. We will accept nothing less than full Victory!

Good Luck! And let us all beseech the blessing of Almighty God upon this great and noble undertaking.

Dwight Eisenhower

RIGHT
Dwight D. Eisenhower's message to the Allied troops taking part in the D-Day landings. On it, Desmond has written, "We were all there in the first week of the June 1944 invasion," and "112 HAA Regiment workshop Coy."

BELOW
Men waded the last few yards to shore.

remote-controlled bomb—probably one of the first V-1 flying bombs to be launched at the UK; Desmond was lucky to be on an upper level and able to escape by climbing over the debris which had fallen on top of his comrades on the lower decks. He finally landed with the Canadians on Juno Beach, at a place called Le Hamel. But soon after his arrival he watched as the Sherwood Foresters set out for the front in their distinctive Lincoln-green uniforms, only to be brought back that evening as a pile of bodies on the back of a truck.

Desmond's unit advanced to Lisieux, Amiens, and Pont-de-Briques in northern France, where his French language skills were much appreciated by his comrades, who were thus able to communicate with local people. Because of his French fluency, in September 1944, his colonel asked him to deliver a sensitive letter to a woman living in Brussels—a woman named Elly Gelenne. He didn't know what the letter contained, but was simply given an address: 19 Rue du Pont Neuf.

A Rapid Courtship

Desmond had no idea that he was the bearer of a letter bringing news that Elly's husband Paul Gelenne had been tortured before being murdered by the Germans in Breendonk Concentration Camp. Elly was devastated. She showed the letter to Desmond, who comforted her as best he could. He was about to take his leave when Elly invited him to stay for dinner and called Louisa down to join them.

BELOW
Together in Brussels in the winter of 1944-45 after Desmond's proposal of marriage.

Desmond introduced himself as "Paul Henry," as he always did when speaking French because "Desmond" was often mispronounced as "demon" by French speakers. Louisa told him her nickname, "Loup" ("wolf"), pronounced with a silent "p." Despite the tragic circumstances of the dinner, Desmond and Louisa were immediately attracted to each other, finding that they shared a love of French poetry and literature. Louisa was captivated by this gentle, witty English soldier and Desmond was taken by the "utterly charming" French-speaking girl. They swapped addresses, and thus began an intense correspondence.

Over the next few months, Desmond's unit moved from northern France into Belgium and then Holland, and whenever he had leave and could procure transport, he traveled to Brussels to see Louisa. They went to the cinema together, or went out dancing, after which he stayed in a dedicated leave center for British servicemen in Brussels. After one such trip in November 1944, he was making his way back in an army truck to join his regiment, which was again on the move. Just before he reached them, a V-2 bomb hit the convoy. The force of the explosion was such that Desmond's truck was lifted into the air and flipped over, but he managed to crawl out with only cuts and bruises. His comrades in the regiment weren't so lucky and he lost many friends that day; had he been in his usual place in the convoy, he would almost certainly have been killed.

On December 16th, he was once again in Brussels with Louisa when his comrades went to the Rex Cinema in Antwerp to watch a film. A V-2 bomb hit the cinema directly and 567 people were killed, 291 injured. Desmond told Louisa he would have been there if he hadn't been with her. Once again their relationship had saved him.

While he was back in England on leave that Christmas of 1944, Desmond bought a solitaire engagement ring, at a cost of 20 pounds. He had only known Louisa for three months, and in that time he had only seen her five or six times, but already he was certain of his feelings. He proposed to her early in the new year and she was overjoyed and accepted right away. They got married

BELOW
Desmond and Louisa's wedding day, May 19, 1945, outside the Hôtel de Ville in Brussels, 11 days after the Allies won victory in the European war.

on May 19th, 11 days after VE Day, in a civil ceremony at the Hôtel de Ville in the Grande Place in Brussels, where servicemen were allowed to jump the long queue of couples waiting to get married. This was followed by a Catholic church service, then dinner back at 19 Rue du Pont Neuf for family and a few friends.

They only spent one night together as man and wife before Desmond had to get back to his base in Germany. Louisa spent many anxious days worrying that he might be posted to Asia and that, if he were killed, he would leave her pregnant and alone. In fact, it was she who nearly lost her life after falling ill with appendicitis and Desmond who was fortunately able to pay for her life-saving surgery.

Louisa spoke no English at the time of her marriage. She had only known Desmond for a few months...

Leaving Home

Louisa spoke no English at the time of her marriage. She had only known Desmond for a few months and she hadn't met any of his family, so she was taking a huge leap of faith in marrying him, but she loved him so much that she was willing to put her fate in his hands. Desmond had explained to her that they would have to live with his parents until he found work and could afford to buy them a home of their own. In fall 1945, she sailed across the Channel on a boat packed with war brides coming to England to make a new life. She got to chatting with a couple of Belgian girls in the same situation, and they kept in touch on arrival, swapping notes about their experiences in postwar Britain.

Louisa was met in Leeds, Yorkshire, by her new father-in-law and taken back to Desmond's family home, where she would stay in the spare room. She was eager to make a good impression, but found it difficult when she was only gradually learning English. When Desmond's father burped and said, "Excuse my belch," Louisa mistakenly thought he was being rude about the Belgians

ABOVE
After the wedding (from left): Elly Gellenne, Louisa's mother Catherine, Louisa, Desmond, and Jeanne Delbouille, Louisa's older sister. It was the start of a whole new life for Louisa.

(or Belges). Desmond's grandmother asked if she was "accomplished" and Louisa was ashamed to admit that she couldn't play the piano because they hadn't had one at home. She also didn't like English food, except for the puddings, and, all in all, she felt very insecure at first. But Desmond's family soon came to understand what he loved about his caring, lively, and intelligent bride.

Desmond wasn't demobilized until late 1945, when he came back to Leeds, and in the summer of 1946 was able to whisk Louisa off for a belated honeymoon in Torquay on England's southwest coast. He had been thinking of training as a primary schoolteacher, but Colonel Leigh, the head of his regiment, had recognized how clever he was and suggested that he apply for a bursary available to ex-servicemen who wanted to go to university but whose qualifications didn't meet

GERMANY'S V ROCKETS

Working in a base at Peenemünde on the Baltic coast, rocket scientist Wernher von Braun developed a new range of unmanned flying bombs for Germany. The first V-1 rockets were fired at London on June 13, 1944, and had a range of 125 miles and warheads weighing 1,875 pounds. V-2 rockets were even more deadly, with a range of 200 miles and 2,200-pound warheads, and they flew so fast and so high that they were almost impossible to shoot down. Over the next year, 33,000 people would be killed or injured by V rockets fired at England and many more died on the Continent as the rockets were used to target the advancing Allied troops. After the war, von Braun worked on US missile programs, then joined NASA and helped develop the rocket that in 1969 would carry Neil Armstrong and Buzz Aldrin to the Moon.

RIGHT
A V-1 rocket in flight, 1944. They were known by the British as "buzz bombs" or "doodlebugs."

the usual entry requirements. Desmond successfully passed an entrance paper and from 1946 through to 1949 he studied philosophy at Leeds University, obtaining a first-class honors degree, then was immediately offered a teaching post at Manchester University. Money was very tight starting off, but in 1951, Desmond and Louisa were able to buy their own home, three years after their eldest daughter was born. She was the first of three girls altogether and, eventually, six grandchildren.

ABOVE
A drawing by Desmond in Hamburg, 1945: it may be the medieval monh Abolard, in whom he was interested.

During the early 1950s, inspired by his wartime experiences with anti-aircraft artillery, Desmond bought an army-surplus bombsight computer originally employed on bomber aircraft to calculate the time at which to release bombs so they would hit their targets. Captivated by the "peerless parabolas" of the computer's inner moving parts, he decided to convert it into a drawing machine and so capture this mechanical movement on paper. In 1961, Desmond won an art competition at Salford Art Gallery, for which the prize was a one-man show in London's West End. When the competition judge, L.S. Lowry, saw his drawing machine in action, he insisted Desmond include machine-generated pictures in his one-man show. Further exhibitions of machine-generated art followed and Desmond became recognized as a computer-art pioneer.

So while the war brought bereavement and misery for many, for Desmond it meant he was able to express his creativity and achieve academic acclaim while providing a decent standard of living for his family. And for Louisa, it brought her a refined, intelligent, Francophile husband without any need for a dowry.

IDENTITY CARD

ÉTIENNE MICHEL RENÉ SZABO
NAME

HUNGARIAN
NATIONALITY

MARCH 4, 1910
DOB

ADJUTANT-CHEF
ROLE

13TH DEMI-BRIGADE OF THE FOREIGN LEGION (DBLE)
ORGANIZATION

VIOLETTE REINE ELIZABETH BUSHELL
NAME

ANGLO-FRENCH
NATIONALITY

JUNE 26, 1921
DOB

ENSIGN
ROLE

ATS / BRITISH SPECIAL OPERATIONS EXECUTIVE
ORGANIZATION

Étienne & Violette Szabo

A chance meeting in a crowded London street between a young Parisian girl and a Hungarian-born officer was responsible for creating one of the war's most renowned heroines, as well as one of its most tragic love stories.

Violette knew all about wartime romance because her French mother had met her English father in Paris during World War I. They came to live in London when Violette was 11, and at the outbreak of World War II she had a job selling perfume in the Bon Marché department store in Brixton.

By mid-1940, thousands of French nationals had arrived in London fleeing the Nazis, and it was soon decided that on Bastille Day, July 14th, they should parade past the Cenotaph. Violette went along with her friend Winnie Wilson, because her mother had suggested that she find a homesick French soldier and bring him back for dinner. Winnie and Violette didn't want to appear too forward, but eventually they began chatting with a handsome member of the French Foreign Legion by the name of Étienne Szabo. He was delighted to accept the invitation, enticed no doubt by Violette's beauty as much as the prospect of a home-cooked meal.

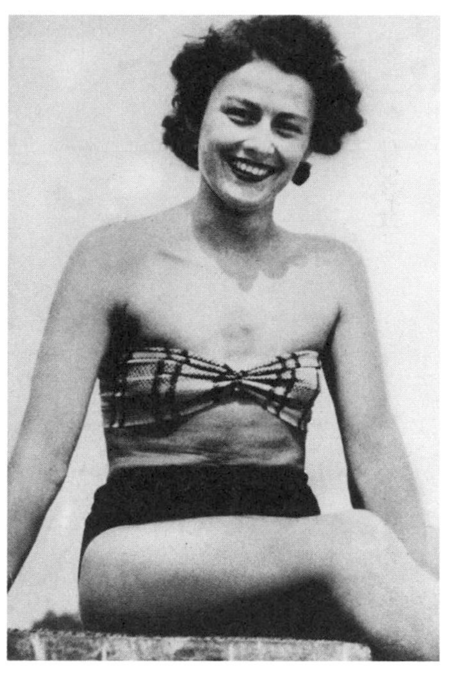

ABOVE
Violette in a carefree mood before the war. She loved sports and dancing.

Over dinner, Étienne told Violette's family a little about himself. Born in Hungary, he had been orphaned at an early age and sent to live with relatives near Marseilles. He'd joined the Foreign Legion in his early twenties and had already seen action in Narvik, Norway, when his unit landed by sea in the middle of a German troop deployment and was forced to retreat across the border to Sweden.

Violette was mesmerized. Courageous and utterly determined that the Nazis must and would be defeated, Étienne was by far the most interesting, exciting man she had ever met. When he asked if he might see her again, her answer was a definitive "Yes."

OPPOSITE
Violette and Étienne were an extraordinarily good-looking couple, who turned heads wherever they went.

A 38-day Courtship

Violette and Étienne met every day for the remainder of his leave, then wrote to each other daily when he returned to base. Within weeks they had fallen passionately in love and were discussing marriage. Étienne spoke no English and Violette's father spoke no French, but Étienne learned just enough broken English to allow him to ask formally for her hand in marriage; at the age of 19, she was technically still a minor, so permission was required. Her parents were shocked by the speed of the courtship and the 11-year age difference, but they could tell that Étienne was a gentleman and knew their headstrong daughter better than to stand in her way.

BELOW
Étienne and Violette on their wedding day. The marriage took place by special license because she was underage.

The couple married on August 21, 1940, at Aldershot Registry Office, Hampshire, and spent a week-long honeymoon in a small hotel nearby, then Étienne set sail for Africa with his brigade, the 13th, and Violette returned to her parents' home. Hoping to help the war effort while Étienne was in Africa risking his life, she volunteered for the post office telephone service.

The brigade made its way around the Cape of Good Hope and up the east coast of Africa before heading inland to fight the Italians in Eritrea, then up through Sinai and Syria. It was a difficult time as they were fighting their own countrymen (see box overleaf), but the Free French forces prevailed, eventually taking Damascus in May 1941.

...Tania was born at St. Mary's Hospital in Paddington—a small, dark-haired girl who looked exactly like her father.

At the end of August, more than a year after his wedding, Étienne was able to return to England to see his stunning bride. She caught a train to Liverpool to join him for a week-long second honeymoon, but the time flew by and all too soon he had to return to Africa. Immediately after he left, Violette volunteered for the Auxiliary Territorial Service (ATS), the women's branch of the army, and started her training—only to find that she was pregnant. It was difficult to get word to Étienne but when he finally heard the news he was moved almost to tears. On June 8, 1942, their daughter Tania was born at St. Mary's Hospital in Paddington—a small, dark-haired girl who looked exactly like her father.

ABOVE
Idyllically happy while on honeymoon, August 1940.

BELOW
At the Battle of Bir Hakeim, Étienne's unit was attacked on the ground and from the air.

By this time the 13th DBLE were deep into the Sahara Desert at Bir Hakeim, under constant bombardment from field marshal Rommel's troops, on both ground and from the air. Though vastly outnumbered, the Free French forces managed to hold back the Germans for 16 days, during which a third of Étienne's colleagues were killed. On June 10th, they were encircled but managed to escape just before a Panzer division moved in and found them gone. Their sacrifice wasn't in vain, because those extra days gave the British time to get their army in place to resist Rommel's onslaught.

When Étienne reached safety, he heard of Tania's birth and immediately applied for leave to come home and meet his baby daughter. But on October 23rd, his brigade was deployed in the Battle of El Alamein. The Free French forces were tasked with climbing a sheer rock face to attack the German and Italian tanks at the top, an almost impossible challenge. According to dispatches, Étienne showed great courage in leading his men into action, but on the morning of the 24th he was badly injured and, when the ambulance taking him to the hospital was hit, he died. He would never know that his actions at Bir Hakeim had helped the Allies to win at El Alamein, a crucial turning point in the Desert War.

DIVIDED LOYALTIES

In June 1940, three days after Marshal Pétain signed an armistice with Nazi Germany, General Charles de Gaulle broadcast an appeal to the French people, asking them to continue their resistance. "Has the last word been said? Must hope disappear? Is defeat final? No!" he thundered. Like the French population in general, the Foreign Legion was split down the middle between those who joined the Free French Army under de Gaulle and those who supported the Vichy government under Pétain. Of Étienne's brigade, the 13th DBLE, 31 officers chose repatriation while 28, including Étienne, elected to form a Free French unit, which would later clash with Vichy legions during the Syria campaign of 1941.

RIGHT
General de Gaulle inspects French troops in Whitehall on July 14, 1940, the day Étienne and Violette first met.

ABOVE
Rommel with the 15th Panzer division. They were defeated by Montgomery's troops at El Alamein and forced to retreat toward Tunisia.

Letters had always taken a long time getting back to England from the desert, so Violette didn't worry unduly at the gap, but after a few weeks without news she began to make inquiries. Meanwhile, she continued to write every day, telling Étienne all about their daughter's progress and assuring him of her undying love. When the tragic news arrived, she was devastated. They'd had so little time together and he had never met his only child. Her grief quickly turned to fury and she vowed that she would do her utmost to defeat the Germans who had killed her beloved husband. Whatever it took, she was determined to avenge his death.

Special Agent Szabo

During her time in the ATS, it had been noted that Violette spoke fluent French, so that, after Étienne's death when she began to inquire about how she could best help the war effort, a top-secret organization known as the Special Operations Executive (SOE) made contact and asked if she would be willing to work for them. Their role was to liaise with resistance cells in Occupied Europe, organizing the delivery of weapons and supplies with which they could sabotage infrastructure, thus obstructing German troop movements, as well as radio sets so they could report on enemy activity. The SOE wanted Violette to operate as a courier behind enemy lines; still stricken with grief, she didn't hesitate to accept. She entrusted Tania to the care of a nanny in London's Mill Hill, and in July 1943 her training began.

Carte d'Identité
Nom Leroy
Prénoms Corinne Reine
Profession Secrétaire Commerciale
Né le 26 Juin 1921.
à Bailleul
Département Nord
Nationalité Française
Domicile 64 rue Thiers Le Havre
15 FRANCS

SIGNALEMENT
Taille 1m 64
Cheveux châtains
Moustache
Yeux marrons
Signes particuliers néant
Dos rect.
Nez Dimensions moy.
Forme du visage ovale
Teint mat
Empreinte digitale
Le Titulaire,
Les Témoins,
5 MAI 1943

ABOVE
The identity card Violette used in France with the name Corinne Reine Leroy. Her profession is given as "commercial secretary." At home, she told people she worked for the FANY (First Aid Nursing Yeomanry), as a cover used by female SOE agents.

Violette was sent to a camp at Arisaig in the Scottish Highlands, where she learned how to read maps, handle explosives, shoot a gun, use a knife to kill, and jump from an airplane. She sprained her ankle badly during her first parachute jump, but carried on with a plucky determination recognized by everyone who met her. When asked, "Why are you doing this?" she invariably replied, "Because I want to kill Germans." It was a simple equation—they had killed Étienne and she would take revenge by killing as many of them as she could.

Training finished in February 1944, at which point she was judged ready for her first overseas mission. She knew she was risking her life, so before setting off she made a will leaving all her possessions to her infant daughter.

On the night of April 5, 1944, Violette parachuted into Occupied France and was met by members of the local Resistance. She made her way by train to Rouen, where she toured the surrounding area to find out what had happened to members of a Resistance cell that had broken up before making arrangements to restructure it. On the way back through Paris, she bought herself some new dresses at the salon of the fashion designer Molyneux before meeting the Lysander plane that picked her up from a field southwest of the city on the night of April 27th. The plane attracted enemy fire on the flight back to Britain, but arrived intact with the mission successfully completed. In recognition of a job well done, the SOE promoted Violette to the rank of ensign.

The Ill-fated Second Mission

Two further planned missions were aborted before Violette again parachuted into Occupied France on the night of June 7th, 40 hours after the D-Day landings had begun in Normandy. The Maquis Resistance fighters she met southwest of Limoges were not as well-organized as she had been led to expect, and it was soon apparent she would have her work cut out in helping them to obstruct German troops making their way toward Normandy.

Perhaps feeling apprehensive, she decided to take a Sten sub-machinegun in her handbag on June 10th when she and two colleagues set out by car to meet the new head of the local cell.

As they approached the quiet village of Salon-la-Tour, they saw a German roadblock ahead. They knew they couldn't bluff their way through, because the guns they were carrying would be found, so they jumped out of the car, firing furiously. They tried to escape through a wheatfield, but Violette's weak ankle gave way and she realized she wasn't going to make it. She urged the others to escape, providing cover for them and holding off their pursuers for 20 minutes until she ran out of ammunition—at which point she was arrested. A German soldier offered her a cigarette and she spat in his face, so fierce was her hatred.

WOMEN SPIES

Some remarkable women worked as spies for the SOE, including Virginia Hall, an American agent who once evaded capture by crossing the Pyrenees on foot, despite her prosthetic leg; Nancy Wake from New Zealand, known by the code name "White Mouse," alleged to have killed a German soldier with her bare hands; Krystyna Skarbek from Poland, who carried out wartime missions in Poland, Hungary, France, and Egypt, and in 1944 talked a Gestapo officer into sparing two other agents who were due to be executed; and Odette Sansom, who was tortured and sentenced to death after being captured by the Germans, but who managed to avoid execution by claiming to be married to Winston Churchill's nephew. All these women survived, but of the 39 female SOE agents sent into France during the war, 13 were arrested by the Gestapo and never returned.

LEFT
Violette was an extraordinarily determined character, driven by her ambition to avenge Étienne's death.

She was taken to Gestapo headquarters, first in Limoges and then in Paris, and some reports say she was tortured during questioning, though she didn't give them a single name—not even her own. In late August, she was herded onto a train and taken to Ravensbrück concentration camp in Germany, then on to a work camp in Königsberg, where she was made to clear trees and dig up solid ground. It was back-breaking work, made harder when the snows came; the prisoners subsisted on starvation rations with no fires for warmth and inadequate clothing for the conditions. Violette made many friends in the camp and did her best to keep everyone's spirits up. She masterminded several escape plans, but before she was able to carry any of them out, on January 19th or 20th, word came that Violette would be transported back to Ravensbrück along with two other SOE captives, Denise Bloch and Lilian Rolfe.

No explanation was given for this journey. All three were given a fresh set of clothes, some soap, and a comb. Violette kissed her friends at Königsberg goodbye, and on reaching Ravensbrück she was placed in solitary confinement. One evening a few days after their arrival, the three women were taken outside and told by the camp commander that their execution had been ordered. The women were forced to kneel before being shot in the back

BELOW
The crematorium at Ravensbrück concentration camp. Prisoners' ashes were dumped in the nearby Schwedtsee Lake.

of the neck, the three of them meeting death with a courage, it is said, that moved all the Germans present. Violette, only 23 years old, was the youngest.

The Most Decorated Couple of the War

Violette never knew it but in September 1944, while she was in Ravensbrück, she was awarded the French Croix de Guerre for her heroism in holding off German troops under fire, allowing two colleagues to escape. In December 1946, one of Britain's highest military honors, the George Cross, was bestowed on her in a ceremony at Buckingham Palace in which her little daughter Tania, attended by Violette's parents, accepted the medal from King George VI himself. Tania's father, Étienne, had also been recognized with the Légion d'Honneur, the Médaille Militaire, and the Croix de Guerre with Star and Palm. Not surprisingly, the combined weight of all her parents' medals was too much for little Tania, so her grandmother had to fashion a neck strap to hold them all up. Mr. and Mrs. Bushell emigrated to Australia in the early 1950s, taking with them their granddaughter, whose memories of the woman who had been her mother were perhaps as distant as soon would be the country she had left.

ABOVE
Violette and Étienne's daughter Tania, weighed down by all the medals that were awarded to her parents.

Violette had become a spy to avenge the death of a man with whom she had only spent two full weeks as man and wife, a decision that may seem impetuous and even irresponsible. But her love for Étienne—and his for her—had been uncommonly intense. The evening before her arrest, she went for a stroll with a Resistance colleague. As they chatted, she told him of her belief that all of life was a chance, that people must take such opportunities as come their way. She added that she wanted her life somehow to make a difference. There's no doubt that both her life and her husband's did exactly that.

...she wanted her life somehow to make a difference.

CHARLEY
JEAN
HUDSON
BAY
ATLANTIC
U.S.A. PEACE – SECURITY OUTPOSTS
GULF OF
MEXICO
WEST INDIES
CARIBBEAN SEA
VENEZUELA
COLOMBIA
ECUADOR
PERU
BOLIVIA
BRAZIL
ARGENTINA
URUGUAY
GALAPAGOS ISLANDS
FALKLAND ISLANDS
UNITED STATES OF SOUTH AMERICA
MEDITERRANEAN
9. To strengthen our position in the Caribbean area which is of obvious importance to hemispheric defense, all possible inducements shall be offered to our neighbors of Central America and the West Indies to facilitate their entrance as equal states of the U. S. A. as outlined on map.
North Ast.
Mag. Var. 1884
Indian Village
Tobique River
River St. John
Lot 40
39
38
Duncan Walker
George Clowes
George Wilson
29
E
D
C
B
A
South 76° 30' East 31 chains
28
27
26
25
24
23
Tracing showing Lots 29 and 38
Range of Lots adjoining the Tobique Ri
the River St John in the Tobique Indi
N.B.
Scale 25 chains to an in

Charley & Jean Paul

IDENTITY CARD

CHARLEY PAUL
NAME

CANADIAN
NATIONALITY

AUGUST 10, 1922
DOB

PRIVATE
ROLE

CARLETON & YORK REGIMENT
ORGANIZATION

JEAN MARIE KEEGAN
NAME

BRITISH
NATIONALITY

JANUARY 20, 1926
DOB

...on September 1939, as soon as Canada announced that it was joining the war, Charley enlisted.

ABOVE
The Carleton and York regimental flag. The cost of the war was heavy for Canada, with 42,042 dead and 54,414 wounded out of 1.1 million who served.

Charley knew how to spin a good line, and when he fell for Jean he painted a picture of life in Canada that made it sound as though he was virtual royalty. But when she arrived after a long journey by ship, train, and canoe, she found his extended family all living in one tiny shack.

Charley was a Maliseet Indian, raised on the Tobique First Nation reserve in New Brunswick, Canada, at a scenic spot where the Tobique River meets the St. John River. He was one of seven children who lived with his mother and father in a small shack, with no electricity or running water. They lived off the land and occasional federal government handouts, and were educated by nuns at the local convent. There were no opportunities for a young man to better himself on the reserve, so on September 10, 1939, as soon as Canada announced that it was joining the war, Charley enlisted. He had to lie to the army board about his age—he was only 17—but he soon joined the Carleton and York Regiment, a New Brunswick militia unit, and on December 1st was shipped to Britain to begin a period of intensive training.

BELOW
Charley (left) with two of his friends in Coulsdon; they enjoyed meeting locals in their time off duty.

Charley was based near Coulsdon in Surrey and on nights off, he and his friends found their way to local pubs such as the Midday Sun or to dances held at Cane Hill psychiatric hospital. It was at one of those dances in 1942 that Charley noticed a pretty red-haired girl dancing with a friend of his. Between dances, he joined them, turned on his considerable charm, and made sure that the friend was soon out of the picture. The girl told him her name was Jean; she was just 16 years old, while Charley was almost four years older. She introduced him to her mother, with whom she had come to the dance, and Charley asked if he might see Jean again when he next had leave. He seemed like a nice boy so she agreed.

Jean's two younger sisters, Kathy and Mary, had been evacuated to Leeds and her older sister, Pat, was working for the WAAF at RAF Kenley in south London. Meanwhile her father was in Formby, Lancashire, with the King's Own Regiment, so it was just Jean and her mother at home and they often went out together in the evenings. Her mother really took to Charley, who was an easy-going character, and she didn't mind her daughter spending time with him. He was romantic, buying Jean gifts and even singing love songs to her, and soon she was swept off her feet. But, by January 1943, it became evident that they'd been doing more than having a kiss and a cuddle on their evenings out, because Jean was pregnant. She was thrilled about it, but her mother and father were less than pleased and she had to endure a long lecture from Father Tindal at St. Aidan's Church. Charley was delighted because he had fallen madly in love with Jean and as soon as he heard the news, he asked her to marry him. The service took place on April 20th, with Jean wearing a fur stole borrowed from her mother. But there was precious little time for the newlyweds to enjoy themselves, as in July 1943 Charley's regiment was dispatched to the Mediterranean to take part in the invasion of Sicily. By this time, Jean was seven months pregnant.

BELOW
October 23, 1943: infantrymen of the Carleton and York in Campochiaro, Italy. The Germans had abandoned the town as the Canadians approached, but snipers stayed behind to delay their progress.

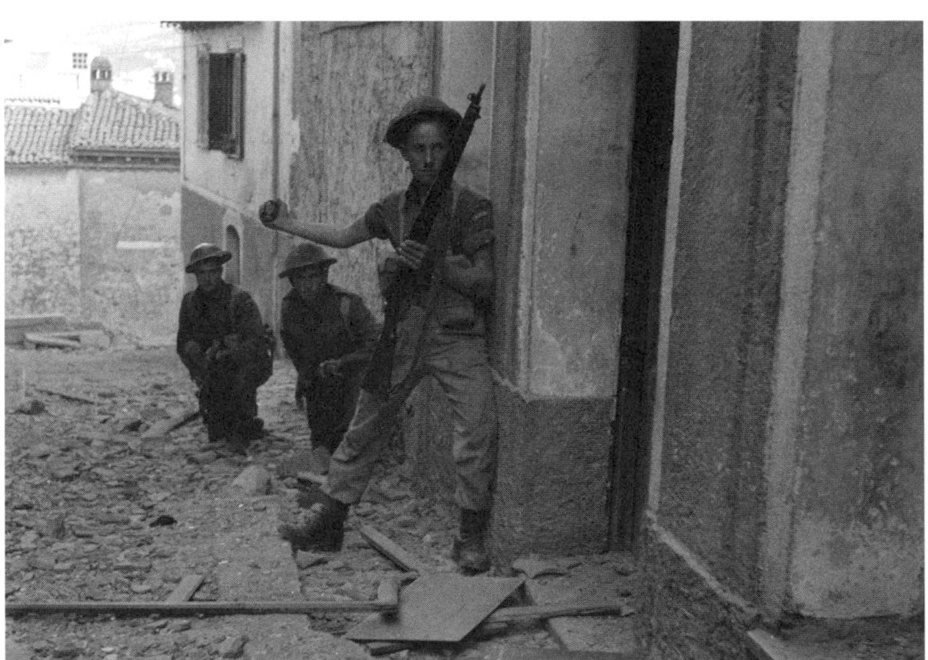

INDIGENOUS PEOPLE IN THE WAR

Approximately 3,000 Canadian status Indians volunteered to serve in the war, including 72 women. Like Charley Paul, they sought economic advancement, a chance to learn new skills, and to see the world. It must have been an eye-opening experience for those like Charley, who had never so much as seen a town before or traveled by ship, train, car, or plane. Some 44,000 Native Americans served in the American military, a higher percentage than from any other population group and, unlike African-Americans, they were not placed in segregated units, but served alongside white soldiers.

ABOVE
Three Native American women in the US Marine Corps at Camp Lejeune, North Carolina, October 16, 1943.

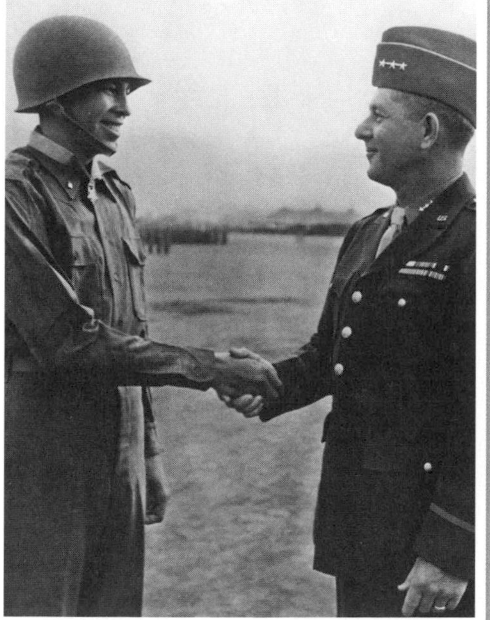

Aboriginal Australians were at first banned from serving because the government worried there might be friction if they lived alongside white men, but many lied about their heritage to join up and it's estimated that at least 3,000 successfully enlisted. All those who survived the war received pensions and educational benefits, but after a taste of life in the outside world, many Aboriginals decided not to return to their reserves, causing a huge disruption to their communities.

LEFT
Lt. Ernest Childers of the Creek Nation, Oklahoma, receives the Congressional Medal of Honor in Italy, July 13, 1944.

From Surrey to the St. John River

On September 9, 1943, Jean gave birth to a daughter, whom she named Christine. A family friend glanced into the crib to look at the baby and remarked, "Oh, she's white!" Jean's older sister, Pat, was astonished, because none of the family had ever thought of Charley as being anything other than white, despite his indigenous blood. Coulsdon was sometimes a target of German bombing raids, so as soon as she was able to travel, Jean took her baby up to Liverpool to stay with an aunt and await her new husband's return.

The Carleton and York had spent July and August as part of the British Eighth Army battling for control of Sicily, where they were frequently aided by the local mafia, who hated Mussolini. In September, they were one of the first assault battalions to invade the Italian mainland and they faced heavy fighting as the German Army tried to contain them in the south. However, Charley was fighting a more private battle, having contracted malaria, and he almost died. He was shipped back to the UK and while in the hospital recovering, was diagnosed as having arthritis in his back and neck, which had been causing crippling upper back pain. He couldn't walk and needed intensive treatment, but in all the months of rehabilitation Jean was only able to travel down from Liverpool once to introduce him to his new baby daughter before he was fit again to return to his regiment, which by now was forging its way up the Italian mainland.

They warned her that Canada wasn't as luxurious as she might be expecting.

With victory in Italy secured, in spring 1945 Charley found himself with the Carleton and York in Holland as part of a brief campaign against the retreating German Army and in the fall was repatriated to Canada and assured that Jean could soon follow him. The Canadian Wives Bureau was helping to reunite war brides with their husbands. Jean visited their offices in London's Regent Street to ask when she could be sent over, and was surprised when they tried to talk her out of it. They warned her that Canada wasn't as luxurious as she might be expecting; the Americans had all the modern conveniences, such as washing machines, and the reserve where Charley lived was in the back of beyond. However, they might as well have been talking to a brick wall. Jean was headstrong and

madly in love with her husband so she couldn't wait to get there and be with him again.

On May 14, 1946, along with hundreds of other war brides, 20-year-old Jean and her two-and-a-half-year-old daughter, Christine, sailed on the SS *Aquitania*, landing at Pier 21 in Halifax on May 21st. They caught a train to the town of McAdam, New Brunswick, where she was joyfully reunited with Charley. The journey wasn't over yet, though, and along with a Catholic priest they climbed into a canoe. Jean clutched her daughter and admired the glorious scenery as they paddled to the Tobique reserve. On arrival they were met by Charley's family and a crowd of locals clustered on the riverbank, all curious to see this white woman who'd come from so far away to live in their community.

ABOVE
The SS Aquitania *served as a troop transport ship during both world wars before being used to transport war brides.*

They walked the short distance from the river to the shack that they would share with Charley's grandparents, parents, brothers, and sisters, and it was at that point that Jean began to get some idea of what she had let herself in for. Their "bedroom" was a corner of the shack with a curtain pulled across for privacy, the toilet was an outhouse, there was no electric light, and water came from a well. It was a far cry from the three-bedroom terraced house in which Jean had grown up. But she loved Charley and knew that she wanted to be wherever he was, so one way or another she was going to make this work.

BELOW
The Maliseet reserve where Charley grew up was at the meeting of the Tobique and St. John Rivers.

ABOVE
The Tobique Reserve, first established in 1801. Jean and Charley's home was down by the riverside.

Life on the Reserve

One of the first problems Jean encountered was that everyone spoke to each other in the Maliseet language. Undaunted, she asked Charley to teach her and by learning a few words a day she was soon able to communicate. Before long, she spoke Maliseet fluently. She had become a legal "status Indian" by being Charley's wife, but she encountered some hostility from the other women on the reserve who were jealous that she had taken one of their men and referred to her as "that white woman." From the start, Jean was determined to fit into Maliseet culture rather than try to introduce her own British ways, and gradually that helped her to win respect.

Life was tough, though. They lived off the land and whatever Charley could earn as a river guide during the fishing season or as a guide during the hunting season. An agent from the federal government occasionally left a barrel of flour and some leftover army rations, but they frequently went hungry. In the fall, they crossed the nearby border into the United States to earn a little money picking potatoes, but it was backbreaking work that was rough on the hands. When winter arrived, Jean was stunned by the fierce cold in that part of the country, where snow lay thick on the ground for four months and there was only firewood to heat the shack. But through it all, her love for Charley kept her strong.

When he took out his guitar and sang to her in the evening, or brought back a bunch of wildflowers from a fishing trip, there was nowhere in the world she would rather have been.

More children were born: Stewart, Nick, Cindy, Lindsay, and then Pamela. Jean gave birth in the convent attended by nuns—there was no doctor for miles around—and it must have been terrifying the first time. Her mother and her sister Mary came over to help when Lindsay was born and were shocked by the conditions. Jean had never complained in her letters home, so they'd had no idea of her lifestyle.

Jean and Charley were better off once his army pension came through, but life remained a struggle. In 1956, Jean's younger sister Kathy married an American and moved to Maine, which was just a five-hour drive away, and Jean was delighted to have a family member within reach again. Gradually their living conditions were improving and by 1962 they had raised enough money to

TOP
Jean and Charley in 1948.

ABOVE
Jean's sister Kathy with Christine.

LEFT
Jean and Charley with friends in the 1960s; by which time Jean had her two-story timber house.

OPPOSITE TOP
A reunion of the extended Paul family in 1977, with Jean standing rear center in a pink patterned dress and Charley in dark glasses beside her.

build a two-story timber house, the first home of their own. Jean's grandfather died and left her a little money, which she insisted on using to install a bathtub with running water—the modern amenity she had missed the most. The children attended the convent school and the family took part in all the annual Maliseet festivities: the Salmon Festival, the Fiddlehead Fern Festival, Aboriginal Day, and powwows in the summer when everyone came from far and wide to eat, sing, dance, drum, and chant.

In 1963, Jean traveled back to England to visit her family for the first time in 17 years. Her sister Mary didn't recognize her at the airport and it was an emotional reunion. In the late 1960s, Charley was awarded the huge honor of becoming chief of the Tobique First Nation, an important role which meant representing the interests of the Maliseet people in negotiations with the federal government. He was instrumental in creating a union of all the New Brunswick Mi'kmaq and Maliseet Indians to give them greater bargaining power and he brought all the chiefs over for a visit to London. But meetings of the tribal council were held in the town of Fredericton, so in 1971 Jean and Charley

OPPOSITE BELOW
Charley wears his wartime service medals and Jean has lace gloves and a black hat for dinner with the Queen in 1986.

LOVE ACROSS CONTINENTS

Many European and Asian women were eager to marry Americans because the United States was a wealthy country that they expected would afford them a better standard of living than at home. Canada was perceived in the same light. Most marriages took place with women from countries where soldiers were stationed for long periods. Approximately 100,000 British women married Americans and almost half as many (44,886) married Canadian soldiers, who had been a presence in Britain from the end of 1939. A total of 1,886 Canadian men married Dutch women, while another 649 married Belgian girls and another 100 found French brides; but only 26 got hitched to Italians, perhaps a reflection of the heavy fighting in Italy that precluded romance and the fiercely Catholic morality that made Italian girls more cautious than others about dalliances with these dashing foreigners. More than 20,000 Americans married German women they met during their postwar occupation of the country, another 15,000 married Australians while stationed Down Under, more than 51,000 married Filipino women, and 758 took Japanese brides. Many German war brides felt marked by an assumption of collective guilt for Nazi atrocities and tried to change their accents so as to assimilate into American society as quickly as possible.

moved there. It was something of a culture shock to be back in a town with paved roads, garbage collection, and telephones, but Charley's arthritis, first diagnosed during the war, had worsened and living off the land was increasingly difficult.

She would have lived anywhere, just so long as it was with Charley.

In 1986, when Queen Elizabeth II and Prince Philip visited Canada, Jean and Charley had such celebrity status that they sat next to the royals at dinner. Charley completed a PhD at Fredericton University and was entitled to use the prefix "Dr." before his name. In 1991, at the age of 64, Jean was diagnosed with cancer. Her three sisters came to visit her over Christmas, but the cancer had progressed quickly and she died early in the new year. All the First Nation chiefs of the area attended her funeral, demonstrating the respect she had won over the years.

She had made many friends among the Maliseet people—but the best friend of all, and the great love of her life, was the man she had met at a dance in Surrey when she was just 16 years old. There was never anyone else, and she never expressed any regrets about her decision to swap middle-class suburbia for life on a reserve. She would have lived anywhere, just so long as it was with Charley.

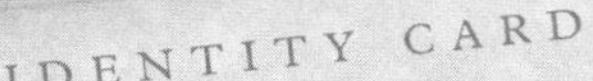

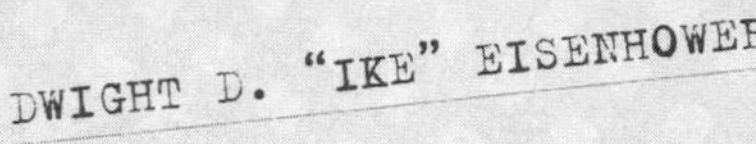

NAME

AMERICAN

NATIONALITY

OCTOBER 14, 1890

DOB

SUPREME COMMANDER

ROLE

ALLIED EXPEDITIONARY FORCE

ORGANIZATION

KATHLEEN "KAY" HELEN MACCARTHY-MORROGH

NAME

IRISH

NATIONALITY

(DATE UNCERTAIN) 1908

DOB

FIRST LIEUTENANT

ROLE

WOMEN'S ARMY CORPS

ORGANIZATION

Dwight D. Eisenhower & Kay Summersby

Dwight D. Eisenhower was based in London for three years as a major general, while his wife Mamie was on the other side of the Atlantic. But he wasn't lonely with the attractive young Kay as his chauffeur, housemate, confidante, and, according to some accounts, lover.

Kay was an aristocratic Irishwoman, born in Cork, who came to London in her late teens to attend business school. She soon got bored and when offered work as an extra in a film, she jumped at the chance, which led to her becoming a model for Worth of Paris. She had already been married and divorced when war was declared in 1939, but she kept her husband's surname, Summersby, when she volunteered for the British Mechanized Transport Corps. She drove an ambulance during the Blitz and was reputedly adept at finding her way through the unlit streets, navigating around burning and collapsed buildings, in order to transport the living to the hospital and the dead to morgues. In May 1941, she met a US Army captain named Dick Arnold, who was in the process of divorcing his wife in the United States, and within a few months they were engaged.

OPPOSITE
Eisenhower on February 1, 1945 wearing the five-star cluster he was awarded on becoming general of the army.

One day in May 1942, Kay was asked to drive for an American general, Dwight D. Eisenhower. She was disappointed not to get someone of a higher rank, but she soon warmed to Ike, as he was known, and in his time off duty she took him sightseeing around London and the surrounding countryside. They couldn't have been more different: he was 18 years older, came from a poor Kansas background, and was a self-made man who'd worked his way up through the military and had a wife and son back home. Kay was 34 years old and very glamorous, even in her shapeless uniform and driver's cap. But they had several things in common: they both loved horseback riding, golf, and bridge; shared a keen intelligence; and were absolutely and utterly discreet.

BELOW
Kay Summersby adjusts the American flag on the bonnet of Eisenhower's car.

Telegraph Cottage

Eisenhower disliked socializing and wanted somewhere he could relax when not working, so he moved into Telegraph Cottage, a five-bedroom house in Kingston, southwest of London, which was on a private drive off the main road. In spare moments he could walk through a gate at the end of the garden onto the 13th hole of a golf course to play a few holes. This would be his base for the next three years, with a New York Irish housekeeper, Micky McKeogh, and his African-American valet, John Moaney. Kay talked him into getting a black terrier pup, which he named Telek—a contraction of Telegraph and Kay. On arrival in London, Eisenhower had written to his wife Mamie of his "rather lonely life" abroad and said that he yearned for "feminine companionship." He had been charged with planning Operation Torch, the Allied invasion of North Africa, and was fully occupied handling the logistics of that campaign as well as the inevitable disagreements among his generals. Soon he began confiding in Kay while they were driving between engagements, finding that he could talk freely to her in a way he couldn't with anyone else. "They all ask to be promoted, or if I talk to the wrong person, what I say is reported all over the world. I know that I can let my thoughts flow with you," he told her, according to the memoir she published at the end of her life.

RIGHT
A quiet lunchbreak: Eisenhower eats a soldier's C-ration by the roadside in Tunisia, 1943.

On November 8, 1942, American forces landed at Casablanca to try to push back German forces in North Africa, and Kay's fiancé, Dick, was with them. Ike asked Kay if she would accompany him when he went to oversee the campaign, and she readily agreed. However, as she sailed out in December 1942, her ship, the SS *Strathallan*, was torpedoed and sunk. Kay was lucky to find her way into a lifeboat, having lost all her possessions. She was rescued the following morning, shocked and in salt-water-stained clothing, and taken to the coastal town of Oran in Algeria, where she was reunited with her fiancé, Dick. They fell into each other's arms and agreed that they would get married in North Africa just as soon as they possibly could. But on that occasion they didn't have long together, as she was soon obliged to travel to Ike's headquarters in Algiers.

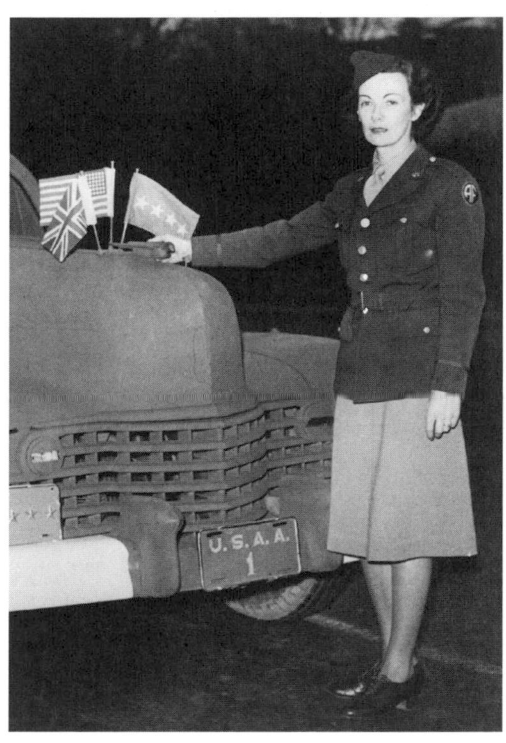

ABOVE
Kay and Ike were back in London in February 1944 when he began planning for D-Day.

"*I know that I can let my thoughts flow with you...*"

She resumed her driving duty, conscious that the enemy was not far away, as cars were sometimes strafed by gunfire from passing planes. Then in spring 1943, Ike called her into his office to tell her the worst possible news: Dick had been killed by a landmine. She sobbed in the general's arms and he comforted her, advising that the best way of dealing with grief was to stay active. In fact, once she got over the initial shock, she realized that she had hardly known Dick. It had been an intense wartime romance, and each time they met had been "as exciting as a first date." Now she would never know what might have been had he lived.

Ike was in overall command of the Allied invasion of Sicily in July 1943, followed by the Italian mainland in September, and had to mediate between Generals Patton and Montgomery, who were often at each other's throats. It was a stressful period for him and

PATTON & MONTY

American General George S. Patton was a tough guy, who lived up to his nickname, "Old Blood and Guts," when he slapped a shell-shocked soldier in a hospital and called him a coward. There were calls for him to be discharged, but Eisenhower valued him and merely insisted he apologize. British Field Marshal Bernard Montgomery (known as "Monty") was an experienced commander with the recent decisive victory at the Battle of El Alamein to his credit when he was asked to collaborate with Patton and American General Bradley for the invasion of Sicily. He found them disorganized and cavalier with the troops' safety, while they found him high-handed and too cautious. Disunity between the American and British forces was further evident after the Normandy landings, when the Americans wanted to push forward faster than Monty did; in the winter of 1944–45, when Patton wanted to pursue the Germans directly while Montgomery favored a more measured strategy; and at the war's end, when Monty wanted to get to Berlin before the Russians while Eisenhower did not. Monty frequently complained that Eisenhower gave American troops better treatment and more supplies than the British. Overall, the British–American rivalry caused Ike a lot of headaches.

ABOVE
"Old Blood and Guts": General George S. Patton in March 1943.

LEFT
"The Spartan General." Field Marshal Montgomery in North Africa, November 1942. His personality and methods were in complete contrast to those of his American counterpart.

Kay later claimed in her memoir that one day he grabbed her hand and declared passionately how special she had become to him. She replied that she felt the same way, and they kissed for the first time. But Ike was wary and apologetic afterward. He said he didn't want to hurt her, but confessed he had realized he had strong feelings for her the night the *Strathallan* sank while he was waiting anxiously for news of her safety. Dignitaries came and went from Algiers—Churchill popped in for dinner, Roosevelt came for a picnic—but Kay claimed that in private moments she and Ike kissed, cuddled, and held hands. He rarely spoke of his wife, Mamie, but confessed that during a recent visit home to the United States he kept accidentally calling her "Kay," which didn't go over very well.

> "The eyes of the world are upon you. The hopes and fears of liberty-loving people everywhere march with you."

In December 1943, Ike was promoted to supreme commander of the Allied Expeditionary Force and they moved back to London, where he was tasked with preparing for the invasion of Normandy. Kay was with him in Portsmouth when he made the decision to take advantage of a brief respite in the bad weather on June 5-6, 1944, and send the Allied Forces across the Channel for D-Day. She helped him to prepare the famous speech he would deliver to the troops: "The eyes of the world are upon you. The hopes and fears of liberty-loving people everywhere march with you." And she was by his side as they waited for first reports back from the Normandy beaches—surely one of the most nerve-racking nights of the entire war.

BELOW
Eisenhower delivers a speech to paratroopers about to set off for the first D-Day assault: "I have full confidence in your courage, devotion to duty, and skill in battle. We will accept nothing less than full victory!"

Plans for the Future

Kay knew that once the fighting was over, Ike would be transferred back to the Pentagon in Washington. The only way she could accompany him would be if she were accepted as a member of the American Women's Army Corps (WAC), then applied for American citizenship. Ike helped her with her WAC application and sent her on a trip to Washington that summer where, bizarrely, she was shown around by his son, John, and briefly met his wife, Mamie. This was the first time she became aware that people were gossiping about her relationship with the general and speculating that they might be lovers. In fact, according to Kay's memoir, the relationship remained unconsummated, although they came close to it on a couple of occasions, only thwarted when Ike was unable to perform. Certainly, Mamie seemed to think there could be some truth to the rumors and was very cold with the visitor from London, although her son was hospitable.

Back again in London, Kay claimed that Ike was more ardent than ever. They couldn't be openly affectionate in public, but he passed her little notes—"How about lunch, tea & dinner today?"—and grabbed any opportunity to be alone with her. He asked Kay if she would like to have a baby and when she said yes, he told her that he would like to give her a son if he possibly could. He worried that he was too old to be a father again, but promised he would do his damnedest. She didn't dare to ask if he would leave Mamie, but that was the hope she cherished.

BELOW
April 12, 1945: Eisenhower inspects art treasures stolen by the Nazis and hidden in a salt mine.

During the winter of 1944–45, Ike became a five-star general and Kay became a first lieutenant in the WAC. They traveled to Europe behind the advancing Allied troops, and Kay was in the next room when on May 7, 1945, Ike accepted the surrender of General Alfred Jodl, German chief of staff, and Admiral Hans-Georg von Friedeburg of the German Navy. After VE Day, Kay and Ike took a vacation in the South of France and were able to relax properly. "Whenever we're together like this, it seems so right, the way things should always have been," Kay claimed Ike told her, and she agreed. He was helping to expedite her American citizenship and she looked

LEFT
V for Victory: Eisenhower poses with his commanders after the German surrender is signed, while Kay smiles in the background.

forward to continuing their affair in Washington, and then perhaps to having that child they had discussed. Surely she must have fantasized that one day he would leave Mamie, a hope that nonetheless she never dared put into words.

The Brush-off

Ike flew home on November 10th, and Kay was booked to follow ten days later, but the day before her flight a telex came from Washington saying that she had been dropped from the list of those on board. On November 22nd, a formal, typed letter arrived for her that read, "I am terribly distressed, first because it has become impossible to keep you as a member of my personal official family..." A month later there was a handwritten note saying, "The break-up of my wartime personal staff has saddened me immeasurably." But there was no further explanation.

Kay was distraught and traveled to Washington, where she contrived to bump into

BELOW
A trip to the theater, May 16, 1945. Eisenhower's son, John, is far left, and Ike and Kay are next to each other.

him, but she couldn't manage to see him alone and in public he was polite but distant. It was only 28 years later, when President Harry Truman's biography was published, that Kay got an inkling of what might have made Ike change his plans. President Truman told his biographer Merle Miller, "Right after the war was over, he [Eisenhower] wrote a letter to General Marshall saying that he wanted to come back to the United States and divorce Mrs. Eisenhower so that he could marry this English woman." The request was refused in the strongest possible terms. His commanding officer had ordered him not to do it.

Looking back, Kay knew that with Ike duty always came first, so if his commanding officer told him not to divorce, he would not have divorced. She also understood that if there were two options, Ike would always choose the path "along which he would do the most good, inflict the least hurt." He was also an ambitious man, and it's unlikely he would have become the 34th president of the United States, as he did in 1953, if he were a divorcee married to the young woman who used to drive him around during the war.

Kay stayed in America, had a romance with a man in California, and in 1952 married a Wall Street stockbroker, Reginald Morgan. She wrote to tell Ike of her wedding and he sent back a note wishing them happiness. She sent him a note of congratulations when he was later elected president. She never spoke of their affair

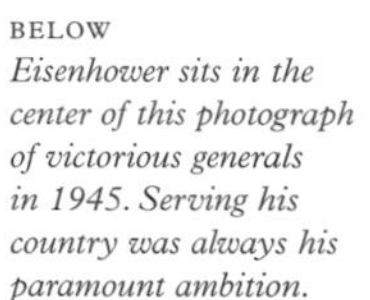

BELOW
Eisenhower sits in the center of this photograph of victorious generals in 1945. Serving his country was always his paramount ambition.

MAMIE EISENHOWER

Mamie met Ike during a family holiday in Texas and married him when she was just 19 years old. The marriage faced early challenges when their first child died at the age of three. Ike was in Panama at the time, and they grieved in different ways, causing a rift in their relationship. As the wife of an officer, she had to move whenever he was assigned a new posting; altogether they would have 33 different homes over the next 37 years. Mamie took to making extended trips back to her family, which displeased Ike, and when she was with him overseas she became involved in humanitarian projects. During the war she lived in a hotel in Washington and didn't see her husband for almost three years. She was reported to be anxious about her husband's safety and upset by the rumors of his affair with Kay. They reunited at the end of 1945, however, and she went on to be a strenuous campaigner when he ran for the presidency and often helped him to rehearse and edit his speeches. As First Lady, she concentrated on entertaining guests to the White House and said she didn't think women should work outside the home, but Ike credited her as being a "shrewd observer" and "a pretty darn good judge of things." When Ike's health deteriorated after a heart attack, Mamie was his loyal nurse and companion in his final years.

ABOVE
Dwight D. Eisenhower with his new wife Mamie on their wedding day on July 1, 1916.

to anyone until she was dying of cancer in 1974 and Ike had already passed away. During her final months of life, she wrote a memoir entitled *Past Forgetting*, about the intense, passionate love she said she had shared with the man who led the Allies to victory over Hitler's troops. Some historians doubted her account: would the general truly have jeopardized his position for an affair? Ike's grandson, David, later wrote that the truth "was only known by them, and both are gone." But it seems undeniable that a strong, loving intimacy existed between Kay and Ike during those war years—one that he chose to end for the sake of duty to his country and to his wife.

IDENTITY CARD

JOHN DOUGLAS "ROGER" WILLIAMS
NAME

BRITISH
NATIONALITY

OCTOBER 13, 1921
DOB

LIEUTENANT CAPTAIN
ROLE

LONDON SCOTTISH / YORK & LANCASTERS
ORGANIZATION

ROSEMARIE GERTRUD BRANDT
NAME

GERMAN
NATIONALITY

JUNE 8, 1924
DOB

A 51. Geburtsurkunde (eheliche

Roger & Rosemarie Williams

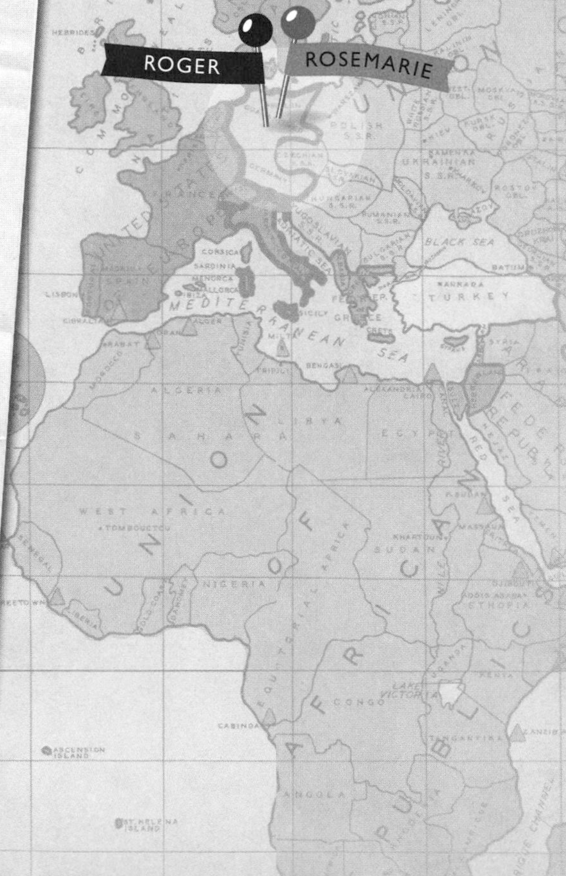

eburtsurkunde E 1

delegen - - Nr. 86/1924)

e Gertrud Brandt, - - -

- - - - - - - - - - - - -

um 1 Uhr 30 Minuten - - -

nschnibbe - - - - - - - geboren.

alter Walter Brandt, wohnhaft

enschnibbe. - - - - - - - -

d Brandt, geborene Heidtmann,

gen, Isenschnibbe. - - - -

: - - - - - - - - - - - - -

- - - - - - - - - - - - -

- - - - - - - - - - - - -

en - -, den 10. März - 1947

Der Standesbeamte

In Vertretung:

ABOVE
Rosemarie and Gisi Brandt with their father, Wilhelm. Theirs was a happy, rural childhood on the Isenschnibbe estate.

Rosemarie was working as a translator in Wolfenbüttel, northern Germany, when one night she saw a drunk British soldier being carried out of the officers' mess by his friends. Little did she guess that her future would soon become entwined with his.

Rosemarie and her elder sister, Gisi, grew up on the estate of Isenschnibbe in northern Germany, two miles from the medieval town of Gardelegen and 85 miles west of Berlin. Their father was the estate manager and they lived in a little house in the main courtyard, surrounded by glorious countryside all around. The estate was huge, with its own brewery and a railway line that brought supplies and transported the farm's produce and beer to market. When the war began, the Brandts were luckier than most because they could live off the land. Rosemarie's father, Wilhelm, was no supporter of Hitler, but he held a prominent position in the local community and wisely kept his views to himself.

Gisi joined the land army and was sent to Bohemia, but she soon became homesick for the north. Rosemarie visited her on a couple

ABOVE
Rosemarie before the war, standing outside one of the estate buildings.

LEFT
Rosemarie, second from left, with a group of friends in a field at Isenschnibbe, June 8, 1940.

THE GARDELEGEN MASSACRE

Between April 3 and 5, 1945, approximately 4,000 inmates from Dora-Mittelbau and surrounding concentration camps were loaded onto trains to be sent to camps in the north. However, air raids had damaged the railway lines and they were forced to stop at Gardelegen, where they greatly outnumbered the SS officers, members of the Hitler Youth movement, and the local home guard who kept watch over them. On April 13th, more than 1,000 prisoners, too weak to work, were taken to the barn at Isenschnibbe. Straw was doused in gasoline and the doors barricaded before the barn was set on fire. Some of the prisoners who managed to escape were shot down. When the US 102nd Infantry Division arrived, they found the charred remains of 1,016 prisoners. Gerhard Thiele, who gave the order to kill, was never caught, but Erhard Brauny, who was in charge of the prisoners' transport, was sentenced to life imprisonment by an American military court.

of occasions, and a local family hoped she would marry their middle son, but she didn't take to the area or to him. Back home, Rosemarie enjoyed chatting with the parachutists at the aerodrome in Gardelegen, but also missed the local boys she used to dance with before they had all gone off to fight. She finished her schooling, studied for a year at a local college, and then worked on the estate farm as they all waited for the war to end.

The Brandts listened with some apprehension to the news on the radio of the Allied advance across Europe in 1945. There were already stories of the Red Army plundering their way through eastern Germany and instigating mass arrests of citizens, so they were pleased that the Americans got to Gardelegen first. German

ABOVE
Bodies found by American troops inside the barn at Isenschnibbe, April 14, 1945.

soldiers hid in the woods hoping to be able to surrender to the Americans, convinced they would fare better than if they were captured by the Russians. There was a lot of looting from the estate and some of the pigs were stolen, so Wilhelm Brandt kept the main gates locked and placed guards around the house and courtyard.

Then on April 13, 1945, an horrific event took place on the Isenschnibbe estate when the SS and various accomplices herded more than 1,000 slave laborers from concentration camps into a barn and burned them to death. The Brandt family were a mile away and knew nothing about it at the time, but a few captives escaped and some local Gardelegers helped to hide them in ditches. Two days later, before the SS had time to cover the traces of the massacre, the Americans arrived and were able to interview some escapees. Even in those days of horrifying discoveries reported by Allied forces on almost a daily basis, the story made international headlines. The Brandts were deeply shocked that such an atrocity should have happened so close to their home, and they couldn't help feeling more apprehensive over what the postwar period might bring.

...horrifying discoveries [were] reported by Allied forces on almost a daily basis.

ABOVE
Rosemarie (left) and Gisi with their father around the time of the war's end.

Rosemarie spoke fluent English, which she had learned at school, and often translated for US Army officials. Wilhelm befriended several of the officers and the family was delighted to be invited to watch Louis Armstrong playing for the troops (see p115). Rosemarie met him afterward and reported that he was "tip-top, very nice." However, the Americans warned Wilhelm Brandt that the area would soon be under Russian control, and in May 1945 he managed to send his daughters farther west to Hildesheim in what would become the British Zone of Occupation, which he hoped would be safer, while he and his wife waited to see what Russian Occupation would mean for them.

A Tough War

Roger Williams from Streatham, South London, was right in the thick of some of the war's heaviest fighting. He signed up straight from school for the London Scottish Regiment, believing (mistakenly, as it turned out) that he had Scottish ancestors. After basic training, in August 1942, the regiment shipped out to North Africa, where Roger transferred to the York & Lancasters. In July 1943, they were involved in the invasion of Sicily followed by the slow, fierce fighting all the way up the Italian peninsula that lasted right through to spring 1945. His unit was "pretty smashed up" at Monte Cassino, with high casualties, so Roger was sent back to Palestine for a period of rest and recuperation at a time when a Zionist extremist group called the Stern Gang were committing terrorist atrocities. One day Roger was talking to a Palestinian police officer when the police car exploded; the policeman would have died had he been in it at the time. So much for having a rest!

Back in Italy, Roger fought in one battle after another and witnessed some appalling sights. At the end of one battle, he and another officer drew lots as to who would care for the wounded and who would care for the horses, and Roger was very glad that

BELOW
From mid-January to mid-May 1944, the Allies struggled to retake the historic town of Monte Cassino from the Germans, and the Benedictine abbey was reduced to rubble.

LEFT
A snowy outing in January 1946. Gisi is on the front of the truck and Roger is at the back, while Rosemarie is between them with her head lowered.

he got the horses. He and a friend nearly found themselves court-martialed in 1945 when they refused to repatriate some terrified Yugoslav refugees, arguing that sometimes following orders is simply wrong. Somehow, they got away with it.

Roger was with the York & Lancasters for the push through Europe toward Berlin and wherever else their orders might take them, but after VE Day they were able to relax a little more. There are stories of parties in the officers' mess at which champagne corks were fired at chandeliers, and much local brew consumed. No one blamed them, though; they'd had a harder war than many.

Meanwhile, Rosemarie and Gisi were finding life difficult in Hildesheim, because threequarters of the town's buildings had been destroyed in bombing raids and half the townspeople were homeless and living in whatever shelter they could find. They heard that Wolfenbüttel was more comfortable, so Rosemarie applied for a job as a translator in the officers' mess there. She was accepted, and she and Gisi found a place to stay with a woman whose husband had been taken as a prisoner of war. They were pleased to find that the York & Lancasters were stationed there, given their reputation for being fair and reliable.

Rosemarie was surprised by the drinking and dissolute behavior as the men let off steam after their years-long ordeal; she later described them as being "very naughty." She first saw Roger drunk and being carried by his colleagues, but he must have made a better impression at their next meeting because by the winter of 1945–46 they were an item. They went skiing together in the Harz

Mountains, went dancing with groups of friends, and soon fell in love. Both were gregarious and fun-loving, with a quirky sense of humor, and before long Roger had asked her to marry him.

Rosemarie had a big decision to make before she accepted Roger's proposal. Would she be happy living in England? Her Uncle Fritz, who used to work in London as a waiter, assured her that she would love it because they had lots of trees. It must have crossed her mind to wonder if there would be any anti-German prejudice after the war, but surely no one could blame her. She wished she could ask her father's advice, but news came through that he had been arrested by the Russians and was being held at

RIGHT
The first German war brides arriving in Hull. Rosemarie is on the second step down and above her is a friend, Ilsa Guest, who traveled on the same crossing.

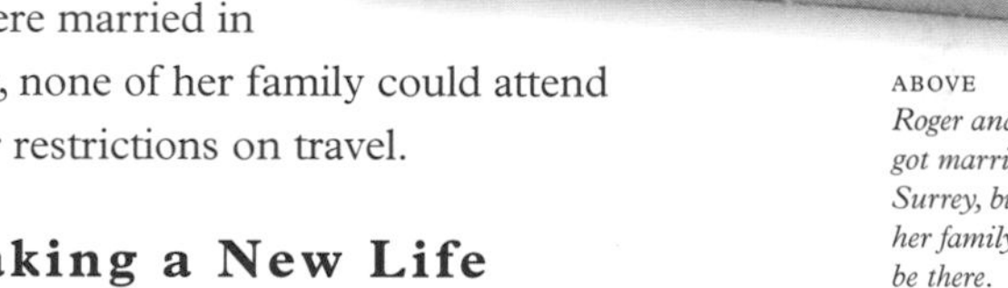

ABOVE
Roger and Rosemarie got married in Wallington, Surrey, but none of her family was able to be there.

Buchenwald concentration camp. As an estate manager, he was an important figure in the town; thus, his imprisonment along with the mayor, the chief of police, and two dignitaries was inevitable.

Roger was demobilized and sent back to London in the summer of 1946 and, having made her decision, Rosemarie followed in October. Her mother came to see her off for the crossing on the Hamburg to Hull ferry that was bringing the first German war brides to Britain. They were met by British press photographers, but Roger whispered to Rosemarie not to make any comment. He had brought a phonograph with him and they danced all the way back on the train to London, utterly delighted to see each other again. They traveled to Wallington in Surrey to stay with his parents, and on December 7th, they were married in the local church. Sadly, none of her family could attend because of the postwar restrictions on travel.

Making a New Life in England

Rosemarie soon found that her fears about living in England were misplaced. She loved the food and the English countryside; her parents-in-law, with whom they lived, were also very welcoming and she didn't encounter any hostility. Her only sadness was not being able to see her own family, because travel from East Germany was so difficult.

A face from her old life soon turned up in Britain. The bookshop in Gardelegen had been run by the Manger family, whose son Werner had gone to school with Rosemarie. He had been injured during the war and was taken to a Canadian hospital in France and then to a prisoner-of-war camp in Norfolk. When Rosemarie heard about this, she and Roger tracked him down. They pretended Werner was Rosemarie's cousin and managed to take him out for dinner on several occasions. When he was released in 1948, before he left Britain, he insisted on repaying their hospitality by taking them for dinner at the Savoy Hotel in London.

Finally, after two and a half years, Rosemarie's father Wilhelm was released from Buchenwald, for which his family was extremely thankful. He was sure he wouldn't have survived another winter there and, in fact, only he and one other of the five dignitaries arrested in Gardelegen made it back home. Over the next decade he managed to visit Rosemarie and Roger, once using a false passport, and on another occasion the Williams family traveled to West Germany on vacation and met up with them there. It turned out that Roger's father and Wilhelm had both fought at the Somme in World War I, and the two of them had a convivial chat about their recollections, comparing notes on their positions in the battle. But this type of contact was rare, and when Wilhelm died in 1958, Rosemarie was unable to attend his funeral.

BELOW
Roger and Rosemarie on holiday in Cornwall: she soon grew to love England.

Roger got a job selling insurance and Rosemarie had several jobs—helping in a school and a hospital, and working in the Sudanese embassy—in between raising their three children. When the Berlin Wall came down in 1989, they were finally able to travel back to East Germany and see Werner Manger and her best friend from school, Elfriede Schulze, but many others had disappeared and Rosemarie was glad she had got out when she could. It must have been hard sometimes to be in one of the thousands of families that were split down the middle by the Iron Curtain, but Rosemarie was always a positive person, and there was never any question that she made the right decision in marrying Roger, who was the love of her life.

...there was never any question that she made the right decision in marrying Roger, who was the love of her life.

BELOW
Returning soldiers are entertained by the Andrews Sisters, Maxene, LaVerne and Patty at Pier 90 in New York, September 29, 1945.

ENTERTAINING THE TROOPS

In May 1941, Bob Hope went to March Field, California, to do a radio show for some airmen stationed there, and it went so well that he spent the rest of the war touring American military bases in England, Africa, Sicily, and the South Pacific. He explained later that, "The reason for our overwhelming welcome from troops all over the world … was that we spelled, more than anything else, 'home.'" Dozens of other American entertainers followed suit, including Bing Crosby, Lena Horne, the Andrews Sisters—and Louis Armstrong, whom Rosemarie saw playing in Gardelegen. Pin-up Betty Grable, "the girl with the million-dollar legs," sent autographed pictures of herself to the troops and replied personally to all the letters she received. The British also sent entertainers to the front line; comedians such as Tommy Cooper and Frankie Howerd got their first breaks performing for the troops. Vera Lynn became "The Forces' Sweetheart" and traveled to Burma, India, and Egypt. "We'll Meet Again," which she performed, was one of the most famous wartime songs.

LEFT
American comedian Bob Hope entertains troops in 1945.

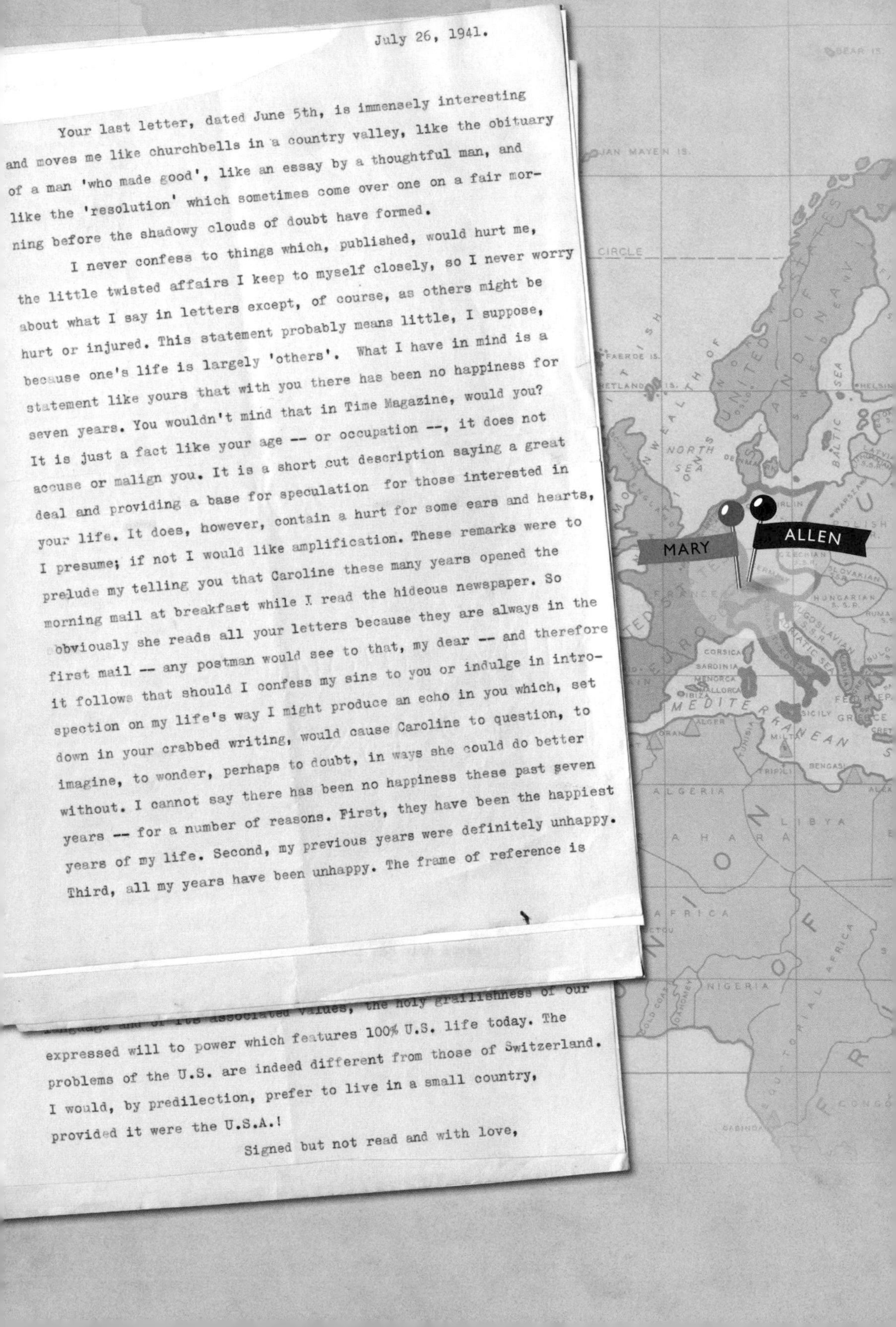

July 26, 1941.

Your last letter, dated June 5th, is immensely interesting
and moves me like churchbells in a country valley, like the obituary
of a man 'who made good', like an essay by a thoughtful man, and
like the 'resolution' which sometimes come over one on a fair morning before the shadowy clouds of doubt have formed.

I never confess to things which, published, would hurt me,
the little twisted affairs I keep to myself closely, so I never worry
about what I say in letters except, of course, as others might be
hurt or injured. This statement probably means little, I suppose,
because one's life is largely 'others'. What I have in mind is a
statement like yours that with you there has been no happiness for
seven years. You wouldn't mind that in Time Magazine, would you?
It is just a fact like your age -- or occupation --, it does not
accuse or malign you. It is a short cut description saying a great
deal and providing a base for speculation for those interested in
your life. It does, however, contain a hurt for some ears and hearts,
I presume; if not I would like amplification. These remarks were to
prelude my telling you that Caroline these many years opened the
morning mail at breakfast while I read the hideous newspaper. So
obviously she reads all your letters because they are always in the
first mail -- any postman would see to that, my dear -- and therefore
it follows that should I confess my sins to you or indulge in intro-
spection on my life's way I might produce an echo in you which, set
down in your crabbed writing, would cause Caroline to question, to
imagine, to wonder, perhaps to doubt, in ways she could do better
without. I cannot say there has been no happiness these past seven
years -- for a number of reasons. First, they have been the happiest
years of my life. Second, my previous years were definitely unhappy.
Third, all my years have been unhappy. The frame of reference is

associated values, the holy grailishness of our
expressed will to power which features 100% U.S. life today. The
problems of the U.S. are indeed different from those of Switzerland.
I would, by predilection, prefer to live in a small country,
provided it were the U.S.A.!

Signed but not read and with love,

Allen Dulles & Mary Bancroft

IDENTITY CARD

WORLD · LOVE STORIES

ALLEN WELSH DULLES
NAME

AMERICAN
NATIONALITY

APRIL 7, 1893
DOB

SWISS DIRECTOR
ROLE

US OFFICE OF STRATEGIC SERVICES (OSS)
ORGANIZATION

WORLD · LOVE STORIES

MARY BANCROFT
NAME

AMERICAN
NATIONALITY

OCTOBER 29, 1903
DOB

INTELLIGENCE AGENT
ROLE

US OFFICE OF STRATEGIC SERVICES (OSS)
ORGANIZATION

ABOVE
Shrewd, ambitious, and highly sexed, Allen Dulles never let his marriage stand in the way of his conquests.

OPPOSITE
Mary's "coming out" is announced in the Cambridge Chronicle, *October 15, 1921. There was a* thé dansant *at their house, at which a small orchestra played.*

"It should work out very well," said spymaster Allen to his new recruit, Mary, on what was only their third meeting, before anything had happened between them. "We can let the work cover the romance—and the romance cover the work."

Mary was the daughter of an upper-class, Harvard-trained lawyer father who suffered from a depressive illness, and a poor Irish mother who had died giving birth to her. She had a difficult relationship with the woman her father married next, but was close to her stepmother's father, Clarence Barron, owner of *The Wall Street Journal*. Barron encouraged young Mary to study people of all types, even "gamblers and crooks." It was advice she took to heart and that would stand her in good stead later in life.

COMING OUT PARTY

Mr. and Mrs. Hugh Bancroft will present their daughter, Miss Mary Bancroft, at a tea at their house, 352 Beacon street, on November 11. Later in the season they will give a dance for her at the Brookline Country club. Mr. and Mrs. Bancroft and their family have returned to town for the winter from "Oaks Farm," their summer place at Cohasset.

MISS MARY BANCROFT

Mary was a clever but restless teenager, who had no trouble attracting men with her lively wit and shapely legs. She dropped out of Smith College, Massachusetts, after a year and at the age of 18 married a friend from school days, Sherwin Badger, of whom she soon grew bored. It was an era in which, she later wrote, "there was plenty of experimenting with different partners," though they did it discreetly. Tragedy struck when their first baby died of fever, but two more followed—a son, Sherwin Jr., and a daughter she named Mary Jane. Then she fell in love with a pianist called Leopold Godowsky and, by the summer of 1933, after 12 years, her first marriage was over.

It was an era in which, she later wrote, "there was plenty of experimenting with different partners..."

Leopold decided not to leave his wife for her but, in any case, within months Mary had met the man who would become husband number two, a Swiss accountant called Jean Rufenacht. She wasn't remotely in love with him but thought he would at least be good to her—a hope she realized was futile after the first time he knocked her out cold during an argument. Despite her misgivings, she traveled to Switzerland with Jean in 1934, only to receive the terrible news during the voyage that her father had succumbed to his depression and committed suicide.

She and Jean married and set up home in Zurich. Mary began to study the teachings of the psychoanalyst Carl Jung, in an attempt to shed light on her own complex psyche and the emotional traumas she'd been through. She ended up in analysis with the great man himself and soon became a strong advocate of his methods. Her husband was away from home on business for long stretches, and she passed the time by perfecting her French and German, writing a novel, and taking lovers.

During trips into Nazi Germany in the late 1930s, Mary was horrified to see the repressive regime at close quarters and was distressed when the fighting began, but in the end she decided to stay in neutral Switzerland for the duration of the war. In the spring of 1942, she was asked by Gerald Mayer of the American Legation in Bern to write analyses of Nazi speeches and articles in the German media, to which she happily agreed, pleased to be able to contribute to the American war effort in some small way.

BELOW
One of the portents of coming war—German troops march into the Rhineland on March 7, 1936.

"Scores of Affairs"

BELOW
Government minister Peter A. Jay with Allen Dulles (right) at the State Department in 1947, the year the CIA began operations.

Allen came from a family immersed in politics and religion: one of his grandfathers and an uncle were both US secretaries of state, while his father and his other grandfather were Presbyterian ministers. He graduated from Princeton University and went into diplomatic service, serving in several European countries, before returning to the States to earn a law degree in 1926. He accepted a job with the prestigious law firm Sullivan & Cromwell, and during the course of his work for them in the 1930s met Hitler and Mussolini and observed what was happening in their countries. When war began, he was one of those who argued vociferously that the United States could not remain neutral, and he personally helped a number of Jews to escape from Germany to the United States.

Allen was an extremely charming man, with a knack for making people like him. In 1920, he had married Clover Todd, the daughter of a professor at Columbia University, but he was wildly unfaithful to her throughout their marriage. His sister estimated that he slept with "at least a hundred" other women and made no attempt to hide the affairs from his wife. Instead, he wrote to her about them in letters home from foreign trips: there was "a rather good-looking" English woman with whom he "danced and drank champagne till quite late" and "an attractive (not beautiful) Irish-French female" with whom he stayed "till the early hours." In one letter to Clover, he confessed he didn't deserve her, as he was "rather too fond of the company of other ladies." But for some reason she put up with his behavior.

...he was "rather too fond of the company of other ladies."

In June 1942, the Office of Strategic Services (OSS) was formed—an intelligence agency designed to coordinate all espionage behind enemy lines and direct their information to help the military services. Allen was appointed head of the Swiss operation and sent to Bern, where he lived at Herrengasse 23 for the duration of the war. One of his first tasks was to find volunteer recruits who would help to interview the thousands of refugees pouring into Switzerland from all over Europe. He was impressed by the insightful analyses written by Mary and asked to meet her for drinks early in December 1942 at Zurich's Hotel Baur am Lac. He sized her up quickly at that meeting, judged her to be articulate and attractive, and offered her the job of intelligence agent, which she was more than happy to accept.

A few days later, Allen invited Mary to dinner at his hotel and during the evening asked if he could borrow some bed linen as his new apartment had none. When he came to pick up the linen, he made his announcement, "We can let the work cover the romance—and the romance cover the work." Mary was surprised and wondered, "What romance?" But she was delighted to become his mistress as well as his spy. Her marriage to Jean was on the rocks and Allen's wife was back in the United States; they were attracted to each other and nothing stood in their way. Their affair began.

Espionage Swiss-style

Mary and Allen slipped into a routine of speaking on the telephone every morning at 9:20 a.m., when he briefed her on her rendezvous for the day, using a combination of American slang and ridiculous names for people that only they would understand. Once a week she traveled by train to Bern, checked into a hotel near the station, then took a taxi to Allen's apartment, where they spent the day preparing a briefing for Washington. In the evening, he would call in his daily report on a secure radio telephone, leaving them free to spend the night together.

Mary soon fell head over heels in love. "The speed with which he could think, the ingenuity with which he could find solutions to even the most complicated problems, were thrilling to me," she later wrote in her autobiography. She decided to divorce Jean but when she told Allen, he advised her bluntly, "I can't marry you. And I probably wouldn't even if I could. But I want you and need you now." Mary was hurt and disappointed, but admired his frankness and decided that she wanted to be with him, regardless of what the future held.

She soon realized that sex was a physical need for Allen rather than an emotional act. He once stopped by her house unannounced

CODES AND CODEBREAKERS

Allen and Mary spoke on the telephone using American slang terms that would have been incomprehensible to any Swiss or German spies listening in. In the Pacific, American forces relied on Navajo Indians to transmit messages in their own language, which the Japanese could not interpret. Top-level messages on all sides were transmitted in complex codes, however, and the race was on to decipher those used in the enemy's messages. At Bletchley Park in Buckinghamshire, England, in 1941, mathematician Alan Turing devised a machine that managed to break the German "Enigma" code, which gave them the ability to locate German U-boats in the Atlantic and protect shipping. Some believe this intelligence victory shortened the war by as much as two years. In America, in September 1940, codebreakers of the US Army Signals Intelligence broke the Japanese "Purple" code and learned that Japan was about to break off peace negotations—though they didn't learn in time about the attack on Pearl Harbor.

RIGHT
Part of a code-breaking machine at Bletchley Park, outside London.

BELOW
The codebreakers of Bletchley Park. So secret was the work that took place here that it wasn't revealed until 1974.

and demanded that they perform the act quickly on the sofa in order to clear his head for a forthcoming meeting. She knew he had other lovers, too, so when he asked her to translate the memoirs of Hans Bernd Gisevius, a member of the German intelligence service (the *Abwehr*), Mary felt no compunction in sleeping with the German double agent. Gisevius was part of a secret resistance movement against Hitler, and Allen wanted Mary to assess whether he could be trusted. When she reported that she believed he could, he became a key contact for the OSS. Gisevius told Allen in advance about several plans to assassinate Hitler and, after the failure of the attempt on July 20, 1944, Allen helped him to escape again into Switzerland.

ABOVE
Allen with his wife, Clover, July 11, 1955. She was witty, astute, and compassionate, but according to Mary, she and Allen had terrible fights at times.

It was well-known that Allen was an American spy, and it should have been difficult for him to operate freely, but he had some major successes. He made contact with many Germans opposed to Hitler's regime, including Fritz Kolbe, who gave him information about plans for a new Messerschmitt Me 262 fighter aircraft and passed on more than 1,600 documents; German economist Gero von Schulze-Gaevernitz, who would go on to play a key role in negotiating the surrender of German troops at the war's end; and Gisevius, who helped him to communicate with resistance groups inside Germany. Allen also helped in the creation of resistance groups in France and Italy, reported on the existence of a laboratory creating rockets at Peenemünde, in northwestern Germany, found out about the coastal defenses in Pas de Calais, France, and detailed the damage caused by Allied bombing raids.

Mary's affair with Allen continued until fall 1944 when, after the liberation of France, Allen's wife, Clover, was able to join him in Bern. Soon after Clover arrived, Allen invited Mary to meet her and, much to her surprise, she found she liked her lover's wife very much indeed. It didn't take Clover long to assess the situation and she said to Mary, "I want you to know that I can see how much you and Allen care for each other—and I approve." They became friends for life, but that was the only time Mary's affair with Allen was referred to by either one.

Sterbeurkunde G 1

(Standesamt Bamberg Nr. 989/1951.)

Der Oberst Klaus Philipp Maria Schenk
Graf von Stauffenberg,
römisch-katholisch,
wohnhaft in Bamberg, Schützenstraße 20,
ist am 20. Juli 1944 Stunde unbekannt um Uhr Minuten
in Berlin W 35, Bendlerstraße 14
verstorben.
Der Verstorbene war geboren am 15. November 1907 in Jettingen,
Kreis Günzburg,
(Standesamt daselbst Nr. 65/1907)
Vater: Alfred Schenk Graf von Stauffenberg,
Mutter: Karoline Schenk Gräfin von Stauffenberg,
geborene Gräfin Üxküll-Gyllenband.
Der Verstorbene war ~~nicht~~ – verheiratet mit Nina Magdalena
Elisabeth Vera Lydia Herta Schenk Gräfin von
Stauffenberg, geborenen Freiin von Lerchenfeld,
wohnhaft in Lautlingen, Kreis Balingen.

Bamberg, den 14. November 1951.

Der Standesbeamte
In Vertretung

Gebührenfrei.

Pfennig Gebühr bezahlt Nr.
4. Ausfertigung.

ABOVE
The death certificate of Claus von Stauffenberg, executed after the failure of his plot to kill Hitler.

THE PLOT TO ASSASSINATE HITLER

There had been many plans among resistance operatives in Germany to kill the Führer. In November 1939, a bomb was placed in a hall where he was speaking, but it detonated after he had left. After the defeat at the Battle of Stalingrad in 1943, when it became obvious that Germany could not win the war, several officers began to plot among themselves. One of these, Claus von Stauffenberg came to the fore when he was appointed a chief of staff to Hitler on July 1, 1944. After several aborted attempts, on July 20th he placed a briefcase containing a bomb near Hitler at a meeting in his Prussian headquarters, then excused himself to make a telephone call. The bomb went off, killing three and injuring 11, but Hitler merely suffered a burst eardrum. Most of the plotters, including von Stauffenberg, were shot the next day and thousands more suspected of resistance were rounded up by the Gestapo. One side effect of the failed plot was to destroy most of Allen's network of contacts in Germany, as so many of them were executed.

In January 1945, Allen and Clover went to Ascona on the Swiss-Italian border and met SS General Karl Wolff for secret negotiations over the surrender of German troops in Italy. Clover was not allowed to be party to his work in the way that Mary had been and, so that the men could talk in peace, she was sent out in a rowboat on Lake Maggiore, Italy, while they confirmed the details of what became known as Operation Sunrise.

Weeks later, Mary and Clover traveled together to Kreuzlingen on the Swiss-German border and looked across at all the houses with white flags flying and Red Cross symbols pinned on their roofs. At last they could see that the war truly was over, and the relief they felt was immense.

BELOW
Presidential candidate John F. Kennedy is briefed by CIA chief Allen Dulles on July 23, 1960, about the plans to try and topple Fidel Castro in Cuba.

A Strong Family Friendship

After the war, Allen was made chief of the OSS in Berlin for six months before returning to the United States to work for the newly formed Central Intelligence Agency (CIA). He was made its director in 1953 and presided over several controversial foreign policies: the overthrow of the governments of Iran in 1953 and Guatemala in 1954; a failed attempt to overthrow President Sukarno in Indonesia in 1958; and plots to assassinate Patrice Lumumba in the Congo and Fidel Castro in Cuba. He introduced U2 spy planes and was instrumental in the Bay of Pigs operation in 1961, when CIA-funded revolutionaries tried to invade Cuba. President John F. Kennedy discharged him after that, but he was soon reinstated and later served on the Warren Commission that investigated the President's assassination in 1963.

ABOVE
Hans Bernd Gisevius testifying in defense of an old colleague at Nuremberg in 1946. Mary accompanied Gisevius to the trials there. When she asked if he wanted to go, he replied, "Of course not. Who likes to jump into ice water?"

Mary accompanied Gisevius to Nuremberg in 1946 to hear him testify against Nazi officials, including his boss Hermann Göring. She divorced Jean in 1947 and in 1953 returned to live permanently in the States. The previous September, her daughter Mary Jane had married Horace Taft, grandson of William Taft, the 27th president of the United States, and had been given away by none other than Allen. In January 1969, Clover phoned Mary to tell her of Allen's death from influenza and pneumonia. The two women remained friends until Clover's death in 1974, after which Mary kept in touch with her daughter Joan.

Mary's affair with Allen Dulles had been an unusual one in many respects, conducted in an isolated country during dark times, when they both had important and potentially dangerous work to do. But they came through it with an extraordinary bond of trust and respect that would transcend continents and marriages. It was love of a particularly unconventional kind.

It was love of a particularly unconventional kind.

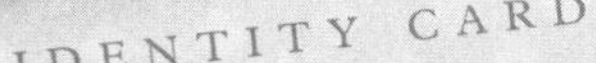

WELDON HUDSON TURNER
NAME

AMERICAN
NATIONALITY

MARCH 21, 1922
DOB

CORPORAL
ROLE

192ND FIELD ARTILLERY UNIT OF 43RD INFANTRY DIVISION
ORGANIZATION

BETTY BOOTH
NAME

NEW ZEALANDER
NATIONALITY

JUNE 4, 1925
DOB

AMERICAN RED CROSS
ORGANIZATION

Hudson & Betty Turner

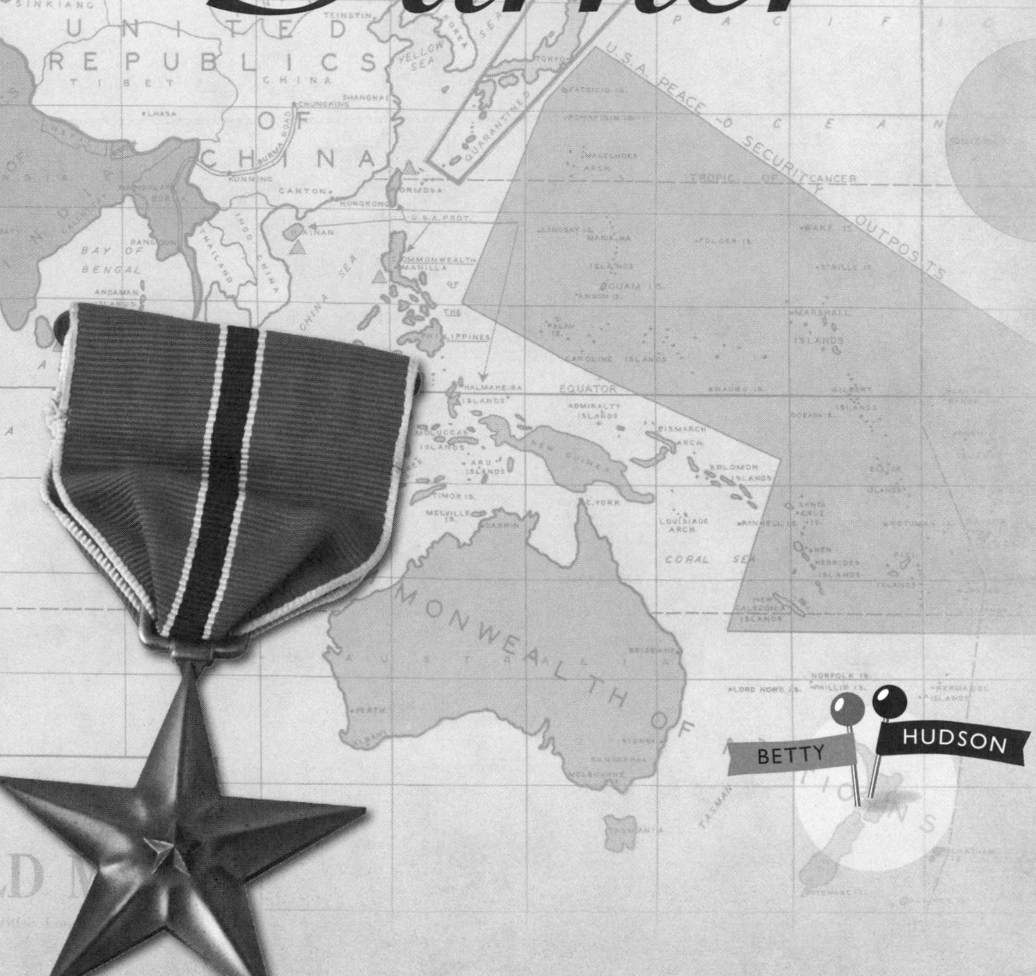

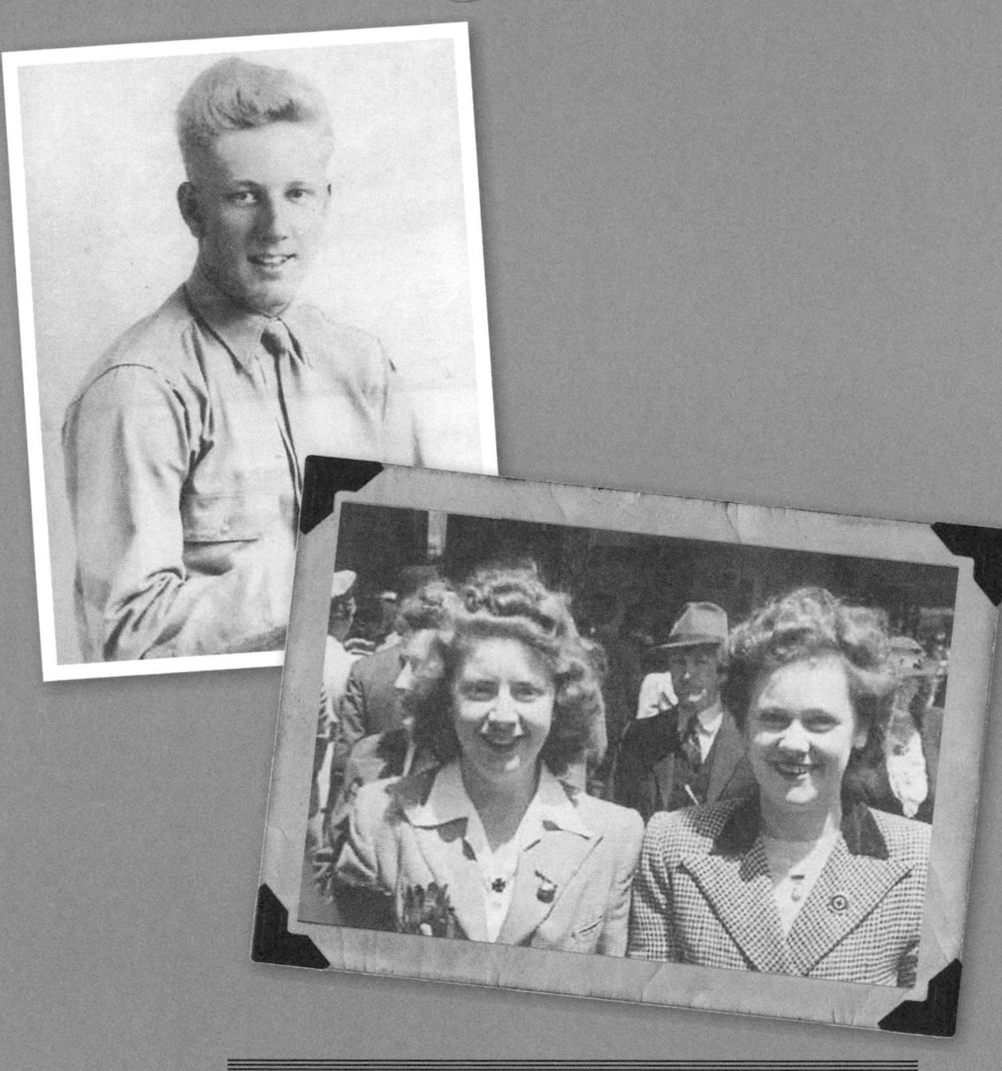

"The Yanks all had the same line, you know. They told me I was beautiful, and I knew damn well I wasn't."

ABOVE
Hudson (top) and Betty (right) with a girlfriend in New Zealand. He was 20 and she was 17 when they met.

Hudson Turner was only 18 when he joined the army, but he distinguished himself in action in the Pacific, coming home with three Bronze Stars and a Purple Heart. Among his many wartime memories, he couldn't forget the cute girl he'd dated during a brief stopover in Auckland.

Hudson was among a group of 70 National Guardsmen who marched out of his hometown of Greenwich, Connecticut, in 1940. He'd been working as an electrician's assistant and knew little of the world, but he learned fast during his military training at Fort Blanding, Florida. After the attack on Pearl Harbor in December 1941, his unit was transported to San Francisco and loaded onto ships heading for Guadalcanal in the southwestern Pacific, where the first major offensive against Japanese troops was to be launched.

"Most of the fellows I went overseas with were from Greenwich," Hudson later said. "That made it a lot easier for all of us because we knew each other."

Halfway across the Pacific, one of the ships in their group hit a mine and sank; as a result, they were diverted to Auckland to re-equip, landing there on October 23, 1942. The young men must have been relieved to postpone their engagement in the fighting, especially given the warm reception they got from the New Zealanders, who were desperate for protection from the looming Japanese threat.

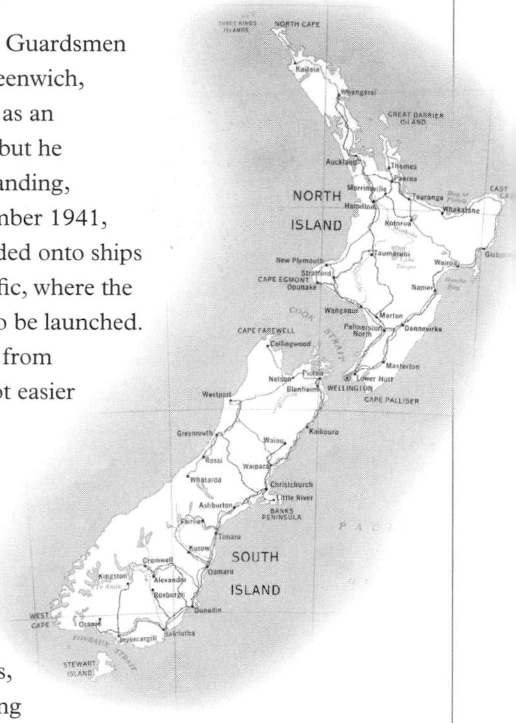

During the first week there, Hudson was put on guard duty outside a warehouse. He saw a girl working in an office above and called up to her, asking if she would meet him at a side door when she finished work.

"All I could see from a distance was that he was blonde and had nice white teeth," Betty remembers. "The Yanks all had the same line, you know. They told me I was beautiful, and I knew damn well I wasn't."

Hudson thought she was pretty, though, and on that first date they found they had a lot in common, including the strange

ABOVE
New Zealand declared war on Germany in September 1939, as soon as Britain confirmed their ultimatum to Germany had expired. After Japan entered the war and began flying sorties over the islands, New Zealanders were keenly aware of how little protection they had.

ABOVE
Betty was bowled over by Hudson. She knew she wanted to marry him from the early days of their relationship.

coincidence that they had both lost a parent at the age of six. Hudson's mother had died in childbirth, and Betty's father had also died young, leaving her with a mother who struggled to raise her on the limited earnings of a hat model and seamstress. Right away, they felt a shared bond. He didn't even mind when he found out that Betty had dated his friend Art before him; at least he got to be the lucky one she chose to see again.

Betty's mother had warned her, "Don't you ever bring home one of those Yanks." They were getting a reputation for womanizing, and she must have been worried that her 17-year-old daughter would fall for one of them and have her heart broken. There were even rumors of some girls being left "in the family way" by visiting GIs. But when Betty brought Hudson home, her mother and grandmother were immediately taken with him. He was respectful of his elders and Grandma Hilda was particularly impressed by the way he always stood up whenever she entered the room, even if she'd only left it a minute earlier.

"Invite him for Christmas dinner," her mother instructed, and so Hudson shared a festive meal with the family. But this was overshadowed by the knowledge that he was due to set sail again just two days later.

On departure day Betty came down to the docks to see him off. There were hundreds of well-wishers present and she smiled and waved just as long as there was still a chance Hudson would be able to pick her out among the crowd. And then the tears came; he'd been so perfect. Despite her mother's warnings, she'd fallen head over heels in love during the three short months they'd known each other. But Betty was nothing if not determined, despite her young age, and she decided then and there that she wasn't going to let him forget her. No matter what it took, she'd do her utmost to stay in his thoughts and in his heart.

Island Hopping in the Pacific

During the course of 1942, the huge wave of Japanese colonization of the South Pacific had been halted by the power of the US Navy and its technologically superior code-breakers, but occupied islands had to be retaken one by one and the fighting was bitter and fierce. Japanese troops dug themselves into caves and trenches and struggled on to the last man standing, while overhead the skies buzzed with fighter-bombers bearing the distinctive red disc on their wings. America had reoccupied most of the island of Guadalcanal by the

BELOW
US troops march down Queen Street in Wellington, accompanied by a brass band: the New Zealanders welcomed them with open arms.

time Hudson arrived, but the Japanese were still trying to retake the strategically important Henderson airfield, and fighting was heavy at a ridge the Americans named "Bloody Ridge" on the airport perimeter. Hudson had been trained to man a 155mm howitzer and also to drive the large trucks that transported them from position to position, so found himself in the thick of the fighting.

By the end of January 1943, Guadalcanal had been secured and Hudson's 43rd Division moved up "The Slot," a channel that runs between the Solomon Islands, to take the Russell Islands without resistance. From there they moved on to Rendova in the Solomon Islands. The Japanese fought fiercely, but the boys from the 43rd were more than a match and were able to raise the American flag there on June 30,1943, with just four American lives lost compared to the 50 or 60 Japanese soldiers that perished.

BELOW
The 43rd Infantry landing on Rendova, Solomon Islands, June 30, 1943. The Japanese garrison there was soon overwhelmed.

Rendova soon became a harbor for patrol torpedo (PT) boats, from where they staged nightly operations to ambush Japanese supply ships. Among the commanders there was a young John F. Kennedy, commanding *PT-109*. Legendary fighter ace Pappy

PT-109

On the evening of August 2, 1943, John F. Kennedy was in command of *PT-109* when his boat was rammed and sunk by a Japanese destroyer. He took a straw poll among his men and they decided they would rather swim for it than surrender. Kennedy had been on the Harvard swimming team and managed to pull an injured colleague along with the strap of his lifebelt gripped in his teeth. It took the 11 survivors more than four hours to reach the nearest island, which was uninhabited and had no fresh water. They continued to another island where they found coconuts to sustain them. On the fourth day after the attack, they encountered some natives who agreed to take a message carved into a coconut shell back to Rendova by canoe. The message read: "NAURO ISL…COMMANDER…NATIVE KNOWS POS'IT…HE CAN PILOT…11 ALIVE…NEED SMALL BOAT…KENNEDY" Finally, on August 8th, all were rescued.

ABOVE & RIGHT
Naval lieutenant John F. Kennedy in PT-109, *and (right) a military report of the boat's loss.*

MOTOR TORPEDO BOATS, RENDOVA

MTBR/A16-3
Serial 0034 (1)

5 August 1943.

DECLASSIFIED

DECLASSIFIED - OPNAV INST 5500.30
BY [illegible] DATE 8 SEP 57

From: The Commander.
To: The Commander-in-Chief, U. S. Fleet.
Via: Official Channels.

Subject: PT Operations night 1-2 August 1943.

2 401

1. FORCE: All available boats (15) on patrol.
2. ENEMY CONTACTS: Five enemy destroyers, attacked in Blackett Strait, five or possibly six torpedo hits scored.
3. WEATHER: Overcast, visibility poor.
4. PATROLS:

AREA B - (BLACKETT STRAIT)
DIVISION B - OFF VANGA VANGA
Lt. H. J. Brantingham — PT 159 — OAK 27
Lt. (jg) W. F. Liebenow — PT 157 — OAK 21
Lt. (jg) J. R. Lowrey — PT 162 — OAK 36
Lt. (jg) Jack Kennedy — PT 109 — OAK 14

DIVISION A - OFF GATERE
Lt. A. H. Berndtson — PT 171 — OAK 44
Lt. (jg) P. A. Potter — PT 169 — OAK 31
Lt. (jg) S. Hamilton — PT 172 — OAK 47
Ens. E. H. Kruse — PT 163 — OAK 19

DIVISION R - EAST OF MAKUTI ISLAND
Lt. R. W. Rome — PT 174 — OAK 50
Lt. (jg) R. E. Keresey — PT 105 — OAK 7
Lt. (jg) R. K. Roberts — PT 103 — Oak 1

DIVISION C - SOUTH OF FERGUSON PASSAGE
Lt. G. C. Cookman — PT 107 — OAK 13
Lt. (jg) R. D. Shearer — PT 104 — OAK 4
Lt. (jg) D. M. Payne — PT 106 — OAK 10
Lt. (jg) S. D. Hix — PT 108 — OAK 16

INCOMING TOKYO EXPRESS
All boats on the stations above indicated by 2130.

At 2400 Division B made radar contact indicating 5 craft approaching from the North close to the coast of Kolombangara Island. Visual contact was made shortly thereafter, by PT 159 which saw 4 shapes in column

3

SGT. HOWARD BRODIE GUADALCANAL
GUYS THAT DESERVE EVERY CREDIT HERE— LITTER BEARERS ON A JUNGLE TRAIL AT THE FRONT— THEY'RE UNDER SNIPER FIRE, TOO + FEW ARE ARMED

RIGHT
Rescuing a wounded comrade during the Battle of Guadalcanal—31,000 Japanese and 7,100 Americans died there between August 1942 and February 1943.

Boyington was also on Rendova at the time Hudson was there and became a hero among the men for shooting down 14 Japanese planes in just 32 days that summer. Everywhere there were ships and planes buzzing around, and the men were kept busy throughout their waking hours, but Hudson snatched whatever time he could to reply to any letters from Betty that got through.

On the night of July 20th, Hudson was sent on a trip to Guadalcanal to pick up more ammunition. He and his colleagues set out in a Higgins boat, a kind of landing craft made of plywood. In the distance they could hear the sounds of Japanese planes "raking the hell out of ships that were taking on wounded," so they moved across The Slot as quickly and silently as they could. Suddenly, a plane appeared overhead, dove down, and dropped an anti-personnel bomb off their stern. If the pilot had had any ammunition left in his machine gun, Hudson would have been dead. As it was, the force of the blast threw him to the lower level of the boat, where he landed on his shoulder and lost consciousness. He awoke to find that he had been carried ashore on Guadalcanal and was lying in a foxhole with a corpsman giving him morphine for the pain.

Hudson was carried on a stretcher to the field hospital in Guadalcanal, where they realized that his left elbow and left shoulder were shattered and his collarbone broken. Two days after the bombing, surgeons operated on his arm before sending him to recuperate on the Pacific island of New Caledonia, where it was decided that his injuries were serious enough to warrant a journey back to the United States for proper rehabilitative care. He was put onto a hospital ship bound for San Francisco, but his ordeal wasn't quite over, because at midnight in the middle of the Pacific, the hospital ship collided with another American ship and both were damaged. He must have breathed a huge sigh of relief when he was finally back on American soil.

Life in Wartime New Zealand

New Zealanders were lucky in that battles weren't fought on their soil, but as a British dominion, the country had declared war immediately after Britain and 150,000 of their young men and women were off fighting. During the early years of the war, Japanese planes were often spotted over the North Island, causing general panic, and as industries were switched to a wartime footing and supplies redirected to the army, there were shortages of common goods. Gasoline was strictly rationed and coupons were needed to obtain clothing, as well as butter, meat, and other basic foods.

Betty worked for the American Red Cross in Auckland, packing parcels for prisoners of war. These boxes were sent to a central distribution point, but most went to Europe, because Japan had not signed the Geneva Convention and prisoners of the Japanese couldn't expect to receive them. After work, Betty traveled back to the suburb of Ponsonby where she lived with her mother, and many evenings were spent writing to Hudson. She sent him at least two letters a week, full of news about her life and anxious inquiries about what was happening with him.

There had always been gaps between his replies, because mail transport was not a top priority in the thick of the fighting, but in July 1943, when she hadn't heard from him for weeks on end, Betty began to worry. And then, at last, relief came as word arrived that Hudson was in America receiving treatment for arm injuries—safe and out of danger, for the time being at least. In fact, for several months while his bones healed, he stayed in the luxurious Greenbrier Hotel in White Sulphur Springs, West Virginia, a five-star establishment converted into a veterans' hospital. From there, he kept up a regular correspondence with Betty.

Hudson was owed some leave, so he went home to spend Christmas in Greenwich, Connecticut, with his sister Eleanor and her husband Kenneth. He was astonished when the local press greeted him as a hero. "The newspaper reporters wouldn't leave me alone," he later recalled. They wanted to know how he had received his wounds and what news he had of other members of the unit from Greenwich.

After the 30 days' furlough were up, Hudson reported to a medical board in Arkansas, which determined that his left shoulder was not sufficiently healed for him to return to the fighting. It was with mixed emotions that Hudson received his honorable discharge from the service in March 1944: relief to have survived the war, but with a sense of guilt that his friends were still out there fighting.

He returned to live with Eleanor and Kenneth and took a job in the post office. Over the next year and a half he dated other girls, but Betty's letters kept arriving and he kept writing back. They had a very special bond and somehow no other girl seemed quite as appealing. And then, in late 1945, he saw an advertisement for a special offer by the Matson Steamship Company—they would only charge $250 for a round-the-world ticket for veterans who wanted to collect their sweethearts from overseas. To be eligible for the so-called "Love Boat," Hudson had to have a letter from Betty agreeing that she would marry him. He was nervous as he wrote and asked her, but pretty sure of her answer. "Anyone who would write me three hundred letters during the war was making a plea to come get her," he said.

"Yanks were forever telling New Zealand girls they were coming back to marry them. Famous last words," Betty quipped. But Hudson actually did. Along with 50 or 60 other servicemen, he sailed on the *Monterey*, arriving in Auckland in January 1946, to be met by Betty and her mother. "He was wearing a suit,"

WORLD WAR II MEDALS

All combatant nations issued their own medals to reward gallantry and dedicated service. In the United States the top one was, and still is, the Medal of Honor, awarded 464 times during World War II. A Silver Star was given for special valor in the face of the enemy, and the Bronze Star, of which Hudson received three, was for acts of heroism or merit within a combat zone. Hudson also got the Purple Heart, for those wounded in action, as well as the Asia-Pacific Campaign Medal for all those who had served out there, and a good conduct medal for completing three years' service. Russia awarded the Order of the Red Star or Red Banner, France the Croix de Guerre, and Britain's two highest honours were the Victoria and the George Cross. Germany awarded the Iron Cross while Japan had a Golden Kite.

RIGHT
The Medal of Honor: the top US military award.

LEFT
The Monterey, *known as the "Love Boat," reunited couples from all over the Pacific.*

Betty remembers. "I'd never seen him in a suit before. He looked pretty good to me."

They were married on March 9th, with Betty wearing a gown made by her mother, and soon after the wedding they sailed back to the States on a ship full of newlywed couples. They docked in San Francisco and caught a train overland to Connecticut, where they stayed at first with Hudson's sister and her husband.

When they first arrived, Betty experienced culture shock over a few issues. Although Hudson had perfect manners, some men weren't as polite and deferential as they'd been back home in New Zealand. And the food was very different. But before long, Hudson got work with Sears as an appliance repairman, and they moved to a nice home of their own in Greenwich where they had four children. Hudson often teased Betty about her New Zealand accent, which she never lost, but he was a devoted dad who liked nothing more than spending time with his family on camping trips.

It was a long way to go to find a bride, and a long way for Betty to travel to make a new life with her husband but, as Hudson said just before his death, "If I had my life to live over, I'd do exactly the same thing." When asked about her ambitions as a young girl in New Zealand during the war, Betty admits she only ever had one: to marry Hudson.

"If I had my life to live over, I'd do exactly the same thing."

AMERICAN RED CROSS
MILITARY WELFARE SERVICE
ALLIED
AIRBORNE
AIRBORNE
TROOP CARRIER
ROSIE
ROBERT
BAFFIN
BAY
ARCTIC CIRCLE
DENMARK
STRAIT
ICELAND
JAN MAYEN IS.
BEAR IS.
FAROE IS.
SHETLAND IS.
HEBRIDES
C. FAREWELL
A N T I C
AZORES
ISLANDS
OUTPOSTS
MADEIRA
ISLANDS
CANARY
ISLANDS
WEST
TROPIC OF CANCER
O C E A N
CAPE
VERDE
ISLANDS
DAKAR
EQUATOR
ASCENSION
ISLAND
ST. HELENA
ISLAND
TROPIC OF CAPRICORN
BALTIC SEA
POLISH
S.S.R.
UKRAINIAN
S.S.R.
BLACK SEA
TURKEY
CORSICA
SARDINIA
MINORCA
MAJORCA
LISBON
GIBRALTAR
SICILY
GREECE
M E D I T E R R A N E A N   S E A
ALGERIA
S A H A R A
LIBYA
EGYPT
WEST AFRICA
NIGERIA
SUDAN
CONGO
ANGOLA
LAKE
VICTORIA
U N I O N   O F   A F R I C A N   R E P U B L I C

Bob & Rosie Norwalk

IDENTITY CARD

ROBERT "BOB" NORWALK
NAME

AMERICAN
NATIONALITY

NOVEMBER 18, 1916
DOB

MAJOR
ROLE

QUARTERMASTER CORPS /
14TH MAJOR PORT
TRANSPORTATION CORPS
ORGANIZATION

ROSIE LANGHELDT
NAME

AMERICAN
NATIONALITY

FEBRUARY 22, 1919
DOB

SUPERINTENDENT
ROLE

AMERICAN RED CROSS
ORGANIZATION

A.R.C.
U.S.
CLUBMOBILE
SUPERVISOR

"I have no intention of marrying anyone in wartime," Rosie Langheldt wrote in her journal. She was wise enough to recognize that the heightened atmosphere combined with homesickness could lead to foolish choices. But that was all before she met Bob Norwalk …

Bob grew up in a suburb of Indianapolis, the second of five children. His grandparents, the Nowaks, had emigrated from Poland and changed their name to Norwalk because at that time it was difficult to get a job if you had a Polish surname. His family wasn't especially well off and Bob worked as a golf caddy during his teenage years, while finishing high school and spending a year at college. He then took a job as a salesman with a precision-tool company and was doing well, making $300 a month in commission, until war began in Europe and he decided it was his patriotic duty to enlist. He went to officer training school in Camp Lee, Virginia, and while he was there an ex-girlfriend called Beatrice kept writing to him. He felt lonely so far from home, and his newly married roommate kept telling him what a wonderful thing marriage was. One way or another, Bob convinced himself that he was in love with Beatrice and they got married right after his graduation, but within a month both knew they'd made a terrible mistake.

They agreed they had to try to make their marriage work, so when Bob was sent to New Orleans with the Quartermaster Corps, Beatrice accompanied him. By then they had a child, a boy called Bobby. They hoped he would bring them closer together, but the sleepless nights and other challenges of new parenthood took their toll. By June 1943, when Bob was told he was being sent to Europe, they had decided to separate, although both agreed they wouldn't divorce until he got back.

When America first entered the war, it was difficult transporting men and supplies across the Atlantic because of the number of German submarines targeting shipping, but by 1943 there was a steadily increasing stream of traffic. In July, Bob arrived with the US Army 14th Major

OPPOSITE
Before Bob sailed home from the UK, he and Rosie had their photograph taken in London in November 1945. Faced with months of separation, she is without her characteristic broad smile.

BELOW
April 1945: Bob (left) and his friend Tom Carver had a week's leave in Paris.

ABOVE
Bomb damage in Southampton—2,300 bombs and more than 30,000 incendiary devices were dropped on the city, either damaging or completely destroying almost 45,000 buildings.

OPPOSITE
October 23, 1944: a large truck driving over a Mulberry onto Omaha beach.

Port Transportation Corps in Southampton on the south coast of England, and it was immediately apparent that he would have his work cut out for him. The city had been hit by 57 bombing raids, the last of which occurred in the month Bob arrived, so that much of the port and city center had been destroyed. However, it was his team's responsibility to bring in roughly 120,000 American troops per month and hundreds of thousands of tons of equipment, and to make sure they all got to the places they were supposed to be. Over the next two years, 3.5 million men would pass through Southampton, and accommodation was often so scarce that they had to "double-bunk"—share a bed with someone who slept at different hours. Landing craft lined the docks while jeeps, tanks, and huge ammunition stores were stowed around the vicinity. All were busy preparing for Allied landings on the Continent, but no one as yet knew precisely when those might be.

Bob was assistant coordinating officer for troop movements in Southampton, making him a key figure in the D-Day preparations. Everything went like clockwork in Southampton—according to port commander Colonel Kiser, "Never did a vessel miss its convoy"—and the D-Day landings on June 6 and 7, 1944, allowed the Allies to establish a beachhead in Normandy. It was a massive logistical success that must have given Bob and his colleagues a lot of headaches in the planning and implementation; but their work wasn't over. There were more troops to send across, and soon after D-Day the first casualties started to flow back to port.

Life got considerably brighter for Bob in August 1944 when a cheerful, very attractive Californian girl came to join the American Red Cross in Southampton. Every morning Rosie Langheldt popped in to his office to find out about ships going in and out that day, and they always exchanged a bit of banter before she went on her way. But he didn't dare ask her out. How could he? His situation was far too complicated.

Volunteering for the ARC

Rosie had grown up in Berkeley, California, with her parents and her sister, Marty. When America entered World War II, she had been working in a luxury goods store selling mink coats and designer shoes, but that felt wrong when men and women were losing their lives overseas. She tried to volunteer for the American Red Cross only to be told that she had to be 25 years old; so she waited and, in due course, on May 4, 1944, a letter arrived telling her she could report for duty. She might have been sent anywhere in the world—the girls weren't told where they were heading even after setting sail from New York—but she arrived in London, England, on July 21st to be greeted by the sirens that meant a V-2 rocket alert.

SECRET HARBORS

One of the problems the Allies faced when planning their landing on the European mainland was that the Germans had heavy defenses in all the Channel ports. So they decided to build floating harbors, known as Mulberries, in Britain and tow them to France. Mulberries were made of hollow concrete breakwaters with floating steel roads on which military vehicles could drive to the shore, and adjustable legs that would be anchored into the seabed. Most work on Mulberries was done in top secrecy in the port of Southampton, the majority of workers having no idea what they were making. Two Mulberries were towed across the Channel on June 9th; one was destroyed in a storm, but over the next ten months the other was used to land half a million vehicles, 2.5 million men, and 4 million tons of supplies at Arromanches in Normandy.

Out of the train window she watched a little plane in the sky "trailing a smoky fiery tail" and counted to ten before there followed an explosion that made her ears ring.

Wartime London was a culture shock. After a couple of weeks, Rosie wrote home saying, "The food so far is fair to dreadful," and requesting that her parents send a food parcel. By the time she got back to her lodgings in the evening there was often no hot water for a bath, and they had to feed coins into a meter to get half an hour of heat. They heard the scratching of rats at night and found the weather depressing even in summer, but right from the start she loved the work and all the people she met through it.

Rosie was relocated to Southampton, where she was trained to drive large vans known as Clubmobiles, which had side panels that could be lifted, allowing the girls to serve hot coffee and donuts to the troops disembarking or setting out. She and her friends would chat with the men, trying to lift their spirits and soothe frayed nerves, and she was obviously good at it because by Christmas 1944 she had been promoted to captain and in August 1945 she was made a supervisor. The job had its difficult aspects: she waved farewell to the crew of SS *Leopoldville* on December 23, 1944, and was devastated to hear the next day that it had been sunk in the Channel with the loss of 763 lives. Also, during that damp, cold English winter she succumbed to pneumonia, but carried on working because she knew how much she was needed.

RIGHT
Autumn 1944: Rosie and her best friend Ski in a Clubmobile they called "The Joker." They served their coffee and donuts through a hatch in the back.

During their training, all the American Red Cross girls had been warned about the "pitfalls and perils" they might face working in places where there were several hundred men to each woman. Nevertheless, Rosie's best friend Isabel (known as Ski) and many other girls fell for the men they were dating. Rosie was the sensible one who advised them to wait till after the war and then invite the men home before making a decision. "If it's really love, it will last," she said sagely. It's not that she didn't date—she loved dancing, and was always happy for the chance of a fun night out—but she made it clear to all the men that she wasn't interested in anything serious.

"I filed him mentally under 'fine type'—some woman is very lucky."

When she first met Bob Norwalk, she thought, "He's a person you can't help noticing," but a friend warned her he was married. As she later wrote to her parents, "I filed him mentally under 'fine type'—some woman is very lucky."

ABOVE
Rosie (center left) watches the "Millionth Yank Ceremony" at Southampton Docks, October 1944. The soldier in question, a private from Pennsylvania, was overwhelmed by the fuss made of him.

The Time of Their Lives

It was January 1945 before Bob plucked up the courage to ask Rosie out. She hesitated before saying, "Sorry, but I don't go out with married men." An older Red Cross advisor called Pop, who knew Bob's situation, urged Rosie to accept the invitation, which would be a double date with her friend Ski and his friend Tom. At last she agreed and they all went dancing at Southampton's Polygon Hotel, where Rosie found that Bob was an excellent dancer. He confessed that his older sister, wanting to improve her own dancing, had made him stand in as her dance partner every morning while they waited for the school bus. It was a fun evening, but still Rosie was worried. Many men were looking on the war as "time out" from their marriages, a chance to "kick up their heels."

THE RED CROSS

Women who worked for the Red Cross during World War II were not nurses, as had been the case in World War I. Instead, they helped to look after the armed services and civilian populations in any area affected by the war. This included sending parcels to prisoners of war, helping them to get word home to loved ones, and inspecting conditions in prison camps. Red Cross volunteers worked in homes where battle-weary troops could go for rest and relaxation, wrote letters for the wounded, and arranged social activities for troops overseas. When the Greek people were starving after the Occupation in April 1941, it was the Red Cross that organized emergency shipments of grain. They were only able to do their work in countries that had signed the Geneva Convention, however, which ruled out intervention in either Japan or Russia. After the war, they helped to locate missing persons and organized transport for war brides to reunite them with their husbands.

VOLUNTEER
FOR
VICTORY
Offer your services to your RED CROSS

It was a laugh a minute, but all the time their feelings for each other were growing stronger.

Rosie and Bob had only been on a few dates when he took her for a long walk one evening and explained that he and his wife Beatrice were getting a divorce on his return. He blamed himself for marrying too young and for the wrong reasons and seemed distraught that it would be difficult to keep in touch with his son in the future. Rosie sympathized and agreed to continue dating him, though with the proviso that they shouldn't get too serious. This, of course, was easier said than done.

They had a busy social life—dancing with friends and exploring the countryside in their time off—and Rosie soon fell for Bob's strong personality and sense of humor. They went to a Church of England service for the first time and heard the singsong chanting, and afterward, on their walk back to the mess hall, he intoned in a high-pitched chant, "Play anybody here a game of dominoooooes…" It was a laugh a minute, but all the time their feelings for each other were growing stronger. They traveled to Scotland, where they enjoyed a romantic stay on the banks of Loch Lomond. For his part, Bob was overwhelmed by this amazing woman who seemed to become friends with everyone she met. And, although she made him do all the running, she was soon writing to her family that she was in love.

At the end of October 1945, Bob wrote to her parents asking their permission to marry Rosie: "I can say honestly that I have never met anyone to compare to her and that I'll devote my life to her happiness." They replied that they were delighted to welcome him to the family.

Four Months to Think about the Future

On December 12, 1945, Bob was demobilized and sailed back to the United States. Rosie wrote in her journal, "The weather this morning matched my mood. It was absolutely miserable." She knew he was going to sort out his divorce so that they could be married on her return—she didn't doubt that for a second—but she missed his lively presence.

At least the days were full, so she didn't have time to mope. She was deeply honored on December 19th when presented to the

OPPOSITE
Red Cross volunteers fulfilled many different roles during the war. Serving coffee and donuts to homesick boys, some as young as 18, was an important morale booster.

Queen at an afternoon party at Buckingham Palace and she was very moved in January 1946 when she visited the concentration camp at Dachau while helping to set up Red Cross services in southeastern Germany.

On the sea crossing back to the United States in April 1946, she mused in her journal about Bob's good and bad points—but the only bad ones she could think of were that he put ketchup on everything, and he added salt and pepper to a meal before tasting it! His good ones included "those eyes that twinkle with amusement as quickly as they glow with love," and his honesty and strength of character. As soon as she disembarked, she caught a train to Chicago to be reunited with him, and they fell into each other's arms. He was able to tell her that his divorce had come through and that nothing now stood in the way of their happiness.

BELOW
Bob and Rosie's wedding on July 30, 1946 in California. His family wasn't able to attend, but they loved Rosie from their first meeting.

First they traveled to Indianapolis to meet his family, who adored her right away, and then they went to California where they married at her parents' home on July 30th. They spent their wedding night in the plush Fairmont Hotel in San Francisco's Nob Hill, then traveled around California before heading back to St. Louis, where Bob had a job lined up. In 1951, Rosie's sister Marty arranged for Bob to meet the Rabel family, who owned the Star Machinery Company in Seattle, and he was offered a position selling their machines and tools. Rosie was delighted because it meant they could live on the West Coast closer to her family. Bob was promoted from sales agent to sales manager to vice president—which his family thought was richly ironic, since he did not have a technical mind and was incapable of operating the tools and machines himself! Rosie got work in Seattle as an advertising copywriter, and they had two children, Martha and Tom. Bob always paid child support for Bobby, his son from his first marriage, but his attempts to see him were met with such resistance that, with sadness, he eventually gave up trying.

For their parents' 50th wedding anniversary, Martha and Tom put together a video of old photographs from their parents' time in Southampton through to the present day, with a soundtrack of their favorite music. After Rosie died in 2002, Bob was diagnosed with dementia and his memory deteriorated, but every night until the end of his life, without fail, he liked to watch that video. He had a tear in his eye and a smile on his lips as he recalled the extraordinary woman with whom he had shared most of his life after their meeting in war-torn Southampton all those years before.

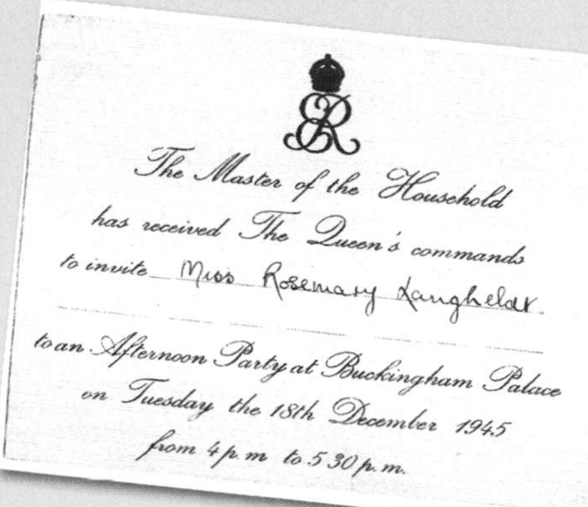

The Master of the Household
has received The Queen's commands
to invite Miss Rosemary Langhelar.

to an Afternoon Party at Buckingham Palace
on Tuesday the 18th December 1945
from 4 p.m to 5 30 p.m.

ABOVE
At Buckingham Palace, Rosie met the King and Queen, Princess Elizabeth, and Princess Margaret Rose. "They were such a beautiful family group, I almost felt dizzy," she said.

LEFT
During her time in Southampton, Rosie collected badges from different branches of the services and sewed them inside her jacket. Decades later, it remained a prized possession.

A TOUS LES FRANÇAIS

La France a perdu une bataille!
Mais la France n'a pas perdu la guerre!

Des gouvernants de rencontre ont pu capituler, cédant à la panique, oubliant l'honneur, livrant le pays à la servitude. Cependant, rien n'est perdu!

Rien n'est perdu, parce que cette guerre est une guerre mondiale. Dans l'univers libre, des forces immenses n'ont pas encore donné. Un jour, ces forces écraseront l'ennemi. Il faut que la France, ce jour-la, soit présente à la victoire. Alors, elle retrouvera sa liberté et sa grandeur. Tel est mon but, mon seul but!

Voila pourquoi je convie tous les Francais, où qu'ils se trouvent, à s'unir à moi dans l'action, dans le sacrifice et dans l'espérance.

Notre patrie est en peril de mort. Luttons tous pour la sauver!

VIVE LA FRANCE !

GÉNÉRAL DE GAULLE

QUARTIER-GÉNÉRAL,
4, CARLTON GARDENS,
LONDON, S.W.1

Raymond & Lucie Aubrac

IDENTITY CARD

WORLD WAR II · MARRIED DEC 14, 1939 · LOVE STORIES

RAYMOND SAMUEL
NAME

FRENCH
NATIONALITY

JULY 31, 1914
DOB

RESISTANCE OPERATIVE
ROLE

LIBÉRATION-SUD
ORGANIZATION

LUCIE BERNARD
NAME

FRENCH
NATIONALITY

JUNE 29, 1912
DOB

RESISTANCE OPERATIVE
ROLE

LIBÉRATION-SUD
ORGANIZATION

WORLD WAR II · MARRIED DEC 14, 1939 · LOVE STORIES

ABOVE
Lucie Aubrac in 1943, when she was working as a teacher in a Lyons school.

The first time French Resistance hero Raymond Aubrac was arrested by the Germans, his wife Lucie helped him to escape; the next time she negotiated his release; then, after he was rearrested and sentenced to execution, she masterminded a daring jailbreak.

Lucie was a clever child. She shone academically, achieving the prestigious *agrégation* in history that allowed her to teach in high schools or at university level, and in 1938 she had just been awarded a fellowship to study in the United States when fate intervened. Mutual friends in Strasbourg, where she was teaching, introduced her to Raymond, who had recently returned from a year's scholarship in civil engineering at the Massachusetts Institute of Technology and was doing his military service in the engineering corps. She asked him about his experiences in America, they started talking, and romance flourished.

Lucie and Raymond came from quite different backgrounds. Her parents were Burgundy winemakers and as a result she'd grown up in the countryside; his parents were Jewish shop-owners in Vesoul, a town in the neighboring department of Haute-Saône. Both had leanings toward communism, seeing it as the only way to resist fascism and racism, and each found their thoughts and feelings reflected in the other. On May 14, 1939, they became lovers, and on December 14th, they married in Dijon.

He warned her that it could be dangerous for her to marry a Jew, but, as she wrote in her diary, "That just made me even more keen."

BELOW
Intrepid, determined, and resourceful, Lucie and Raymond were very similar characters.

Joining the Resistance

In June 1940, when France fell to the German Army, Raymond was taken prisoner. Ever resourceful, Lucie went to visit his brother, a physician, who gave her some pills that would induce a fever. She managed to slip them to Raymond in the barracks in which he was being held; he swallowed them,

THE RESISTANCE

There were dozens of different factions resisting the Nazi Occupation, each one with a slightly different focus and methods. Up to 1,000 underground newspapers were printed and distributed; Allied airmen who had been shot down were smuggled back to safety via so-called "ratlines"; and France's rail network was sabotaged to hamper German troop movements. On June 5, 1944, Resistance groups heard a coded radio message—"The die is cast, the die is cast"—alerting them that D-Day was imminent, following which an estimated 150,000 Frenchmen did their part to sabotage the German Army and slow their passage to Normandy: telegraph lines were cut, railway lines ruptured, trains blown up, and the troops harassed. It took the 2nd Panzer Division two weeks to get to Normandy from their base in the Dordogne, by which time the Allies were well established on French soil.

1er MAI 1943 EDITION SUD Nº Spécial

Nº 27

LIBÉRATION

ORGANE DES MOUVEMENTS DE RÉSISTANCE UNIS

Un seul chef: DE GAULLE
Une seule lutte: pour nos Libertés
Général DE GAULLE

Notre seul but est de rendre la parole au Peuple Français

1er Mai 1943 : Fête Nationale du sabotage contre l'Ennemi

Vive le 1er Mai

"DE L'AUDACE, ENCORE DE L'AUDACE, TOUJOURS DE L'AUDACE ET LA FRANCE SERA SAUVÉE!"

POUR REGNER !

fell ill, and was soon transferred to a nearby hospital run by the Red Cross, from which he managed to escape by scaling a wall.

Lucie and Raymond could then have emigrated to America—he was offered a teaching post in Boston and she could have taken up her fellowship—but they felt it would mean betraying their country. Instead they made the fateful and incredibly brave decision to stay and fight the Occupation in whatever way they could.

The couple moved to Lyons, in the zone that was still unoccupied by German troops, and it was there in a cafe, in the autumn of 1940, that Lucie met Emmanuel d'Astier de la Vigerie. He was organizing a group to resist the Occupation, which Lucie and Raymond quickly agreed to join. At first their resistance took the form of civil disobedience, chalking defiant messages on walls, and dropping a newspaper called *Libération* into mailslots. After the birth of their son Jean-Pierre in May 1941, Lucie worked as a schoolteacher at a girls' school while Raymond was an engineer tasked with repairing the runway at Bron airport. They had a small house on the avenue Esquirol and a maid called Maria. On the surface it seemed a normal, middle-class life. However, this life would become increasingly complicated as the war progressed and their work for the group known as *Libération-sud* became ever more dangerous.

Raymond used four different names—Vallet, Ermelin, Balmont, and Aubrac—and was carrying the identification papers for François Vallet when he was arrested during a routine raid in March 1943. By this time the South of France had been occupied and the Nazi chief Klaus Barbie had established his headquarters in Lyons. Fortunately, the Germans had no idea that the man they held in custody was a member of *Libération-sud*, recently amalgamated with

ABOVE
German officers on motorcycles arrive in Lyons, June 21, 1940, after their division had crossed the Loire.

the seven other main resistance groups in France to form the *Conseil National de la Résistance.* They also didn't know that meetings were often held in the avenue Esquirol house, that fugitives sheltered there, and that Raymond and Lucie distributed packages of weapons and false papers, wrote articles for *Libération,* and were integral to Resistance activity in the region.

Raymond was held for two months, during which time he was regularly interrogated, but he managed to convince his captors that he was merely a black marketeer. Lucie hired a lawyer, but it was only when she paid a personal visit to the French prosecutor that Raymond was granted bail. She convinced the cowering official that she was a representative of General de Gaulle himself and that he would not live to see another sunset if her husband wasn't released. She thought, "This guy is a collaborator and, therefore, a coward. If I speak louder than him, I'm sure to win." She insisted she wanted Raymond home by May 14th. That was their special day, the one on which they had consummated their relationship four years earlier. She got her wish and on May 14, 1943, during a joyful reunion, she became pregnant with their second child.

"This guy is a collaborator and, therefore, a coward. If I speak louder than him, I'm sure to win."

OPPOSITE
Front page of the newspaper Libération, *May 1, 1943. Friendly print-shop owners allowed Resistance operatives to use their printing machines at night.*

The Great Escape

On June 9, 1943, General Delestraint, then head of the *Conseil National de la Résistance*, was arrested in Paris along with several members of his top team. De Gaulle's representative, Jean Moulin, who had been instrumental in unifying the Resistance country-wide, quickly began work on restructuring its upper echelons to re-establish a functioning command structure. On June 20th, Lucie and Raymond brought little Jean-Pierre along as cover when they met him in a Lyons park. Moulin asked Raymond if he would relocate to Paris and Lucie immediately volunteered to go with him, despite misgivings. The following afternoon Raymond left to attend a meeting in a doctor's surgery with Jean Moulin and six other senior figures in the Resistance. He arranged to meet Lucie later, down by the river, but he never turned up. The meeting had been stormed by Gestapo officers and all present had been arrested—someone had betrayed them.

BELOW
A train derailed by the Resistance at Vassieux-en-Vercors in southeastern France. A campaign of derailments and destruction of track was conducted in June 1944 to hinder German troops as they tried to get to Normandy after D-Day.

ABOVE
Jean Moulin, 1942. He always wore a scarf around his neck to hide the scar from a suicide attempt he had made after being captured by the Germans in 1940.

Two days later Lucie summoned up her courage and visited the prison, asking to see the officer in charge. She was taken to Klaus Barbie himself, and she stammered out the following story: she was an aristocrat named Ghislaine de Barbentane and her fiancé, Claude Ermelin, had been accidentally caught up in the arrests while visiting the doctor with a chest complaint; it was imperative that he was released, as she was pregnant and they must marry before her parents realized and her good name was ruined.

Barbie opened a drawer and threw a pile of papers onto the desk between them. Among them was a photograph of her on a beach with a baby by her side. She had to think fast but managed to convince him that this was a friend's child.

"How long have you known the prisoner?" Barbie demanded.

"Six weeks," she replied nervously.

"His name is not Ermelin, but Vallet," Barbie told her. "It's out of the question that we release him—he's a terrorist."

Lucie sobbed and begged but to no avail. Barbie wasn't going to change his mind. Over the following weeks, she did everything she could to make contact with Raymond or any of the others who had been arrested, but there was no word until late August when she was devastated to hear that he had been sentenced to death. Some of the people arrested with him in June had already been killed. She had to work fast.

On September 6th, she acted as a scout on a mission to free four injured agents who lay in the hospital in Lyons. Two of her comrades disguised themselves as Gestapo agents and in that way they managed to get the injured men released into their custody.

Meanwhile, Lucie approached an old German colonel and begged that she be allowed to marry her fiancé before his execution so that her baby would not be born illegitimate. She had to repeat her story to many different people, and several expensive bribes were exchanged, before it was finally agreed that the marriage could take place on October 21st.

The day came, the fake marriage took place and, while Raymond was being transported back to prison, armed members of the Resistance attacked the van and freed him along with 13 other prisoners. He suffered a bullet wound in the cheek, he was much thinner, and he bore the scars of his interrogation by the Gestapo—but he was alive.

Jean Moulin had not been so fortunate. He died on July 8th, soon after his arrest. Some reports claim that Klaus Barbie tortured him to death.

Escape to London

The Gestapo quickly worked out where Lucie and Raymond lived and visited the house on avenue Esquirol, where they interviewed the maid, Maria. Word was sent to Raymond's parents to move to a different address, and little Jean-Pierre was whisked away from the school in the hills where Lucie had placed him for safekeeping. Lucie and Raymond hid for a month in Lyons, then were driven to a safehouse in Pont-de-Vaux in eastern France, from which they moved from place to place over the next few months, looked after by members of the local Resistance. On December 4th, they were distraught to hear the news that Raymond's parents had been arrested; he tried to find out where they were so as to organize an escape, but without success.

BELOW
Messages transmitted by radio were crucial in the unification of disparate Resistance groups, helping them to establish joint strategies and receive messages from London.

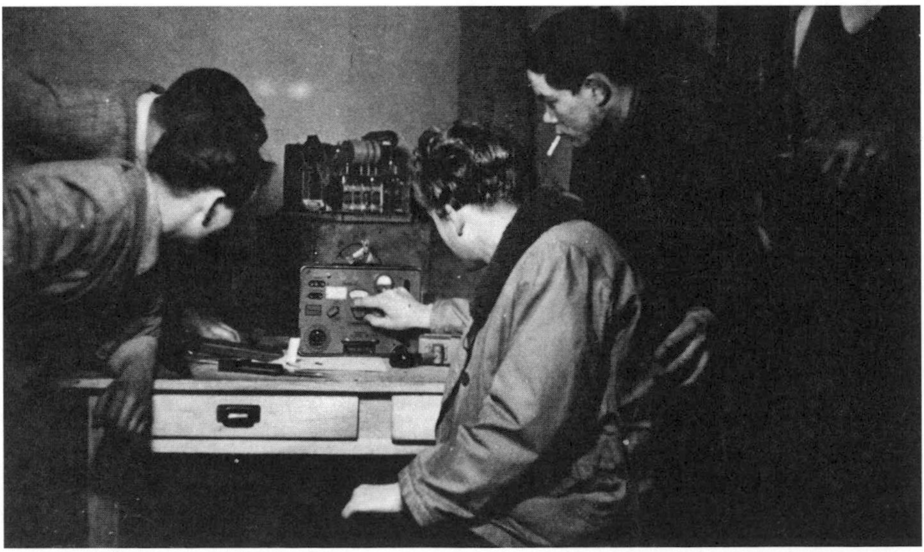

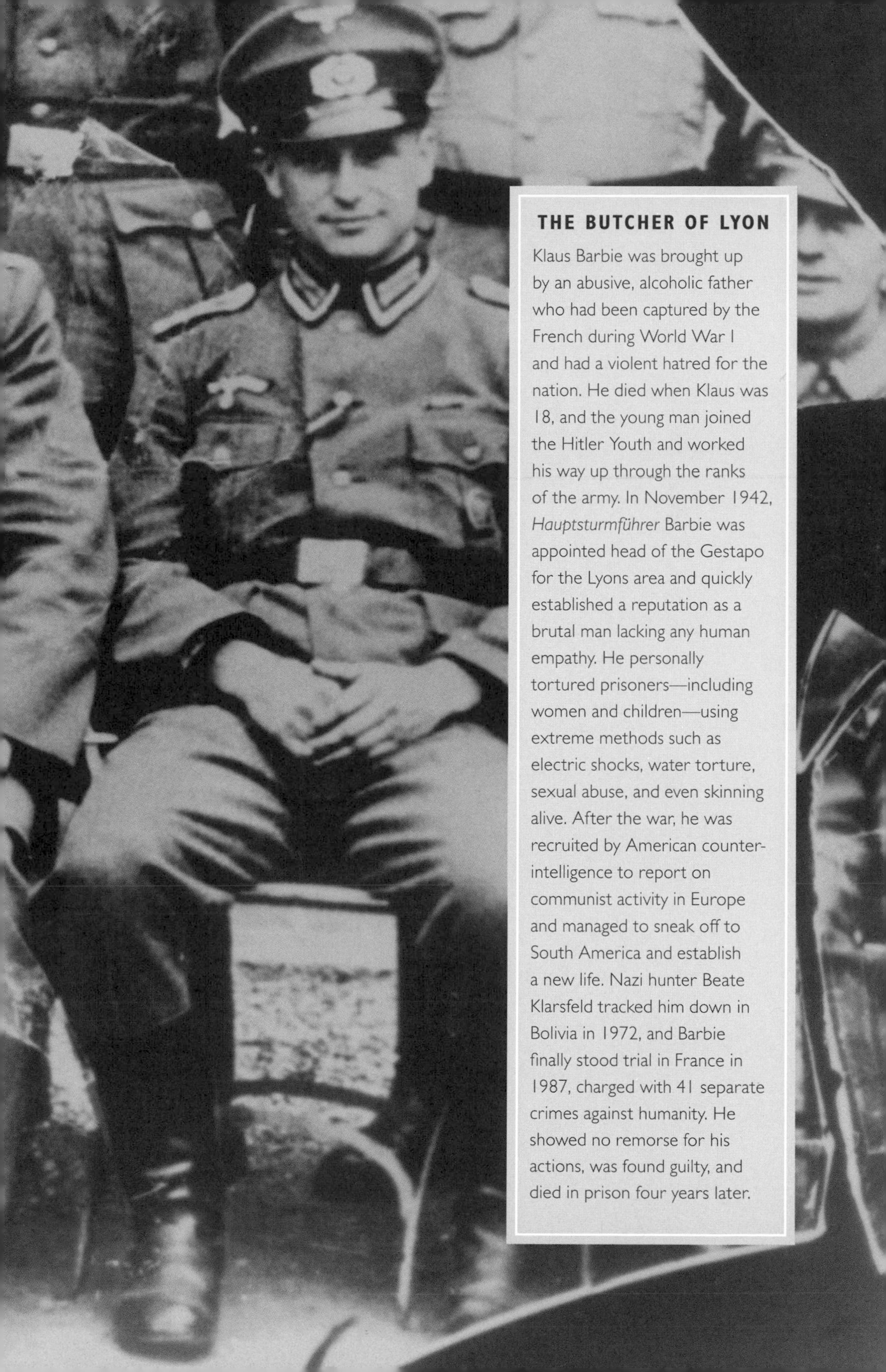

THE BUTCHER OF LYON

Klaus Barbie was brought up by an abusive, alcoholic father who had been captured by the French during World War I and had a violent hatred for the nation. He died when Klaus was 18, and the young man joined the Hitler Youth and worked his way up through the ranks of the army. In November 1942, *Hauptsturmführer* Barbie was appointed head of the Gestapo for the Lyons area and quickly established a reputation as a brutal man lacking any human empathy. He personally tortured prisoners—including women and children—using extreme methods such as electric shocks, water torture, sexual abuse, and even skinning alive. After the war, he was recruited by American counter-intelligence to report on communist activity in Europe and managed to sneak off to South America and establish a new life. Nazi hunter Beate Klarsfeld tracked him down in Bolivia in 1972, and Barbie finally stood trial in France in 1987, charged with 41 separate crimes against humanity. He showed no remorse for his actions, was found guilty, and died in prison four years later.

Listening to the BBC was their only source of news of the outside world, and sometimes transmission was jammed, but they were greatly encouraged when they heard that many of their old Resistance colleagues had been able to join General de Gaulle at his recently established headquarters in Algiers. It was not until the night of February 8, 1944, that they were finally able to flee to England. Lucie's baby was due between the 10th and the 15th, so it was with some relief that she learned there would be a doctor on the flight with them from the little airfield in Villevieux. They traveled through the night and landed at 7a.m. the following morning at an airfield outside London. Three days later, on February 12th, their baby was born—a daughter they called Catherine, Lucie's codename in the Resistance. They had already decided to use the surname Aubrac, one of the names Raymond had used in Lyons.

ABOVE
Vietnamese leader Ho Chi Minh was godfather to Lucie and Raymond's daughter, Elisabeth.

As soon as they could, Lucie and Raymond traveled to Algiers to join the government in exile. General de Gaulle announced that once France was liberated, women would be given the vote, and Lucie was invited to join a consultative body, making her the first-ever Frenchwoman to sit in a parliamentary assembly. In August 1944, Raymond was made *commissaire de la république* in Marseilles, and the couple returned to France. His role was to establish authority in areas that had been liberated, but like many other *commissaires*, Raymond saw it as a chance to purge the police forces of collaborators.

He also did his best to track down his parents, only to discover that they had been taken to Auschwitz and had not survived.

After the War

Raymond and Lucie testified at some of the war crimes trials and were involved in reconstruction committees, but their communist beliefs made De Gaulle wary of giving them too much responsibility. They became so friendly with Ho Chi Minh, the communist leader of Vietnam, that he agreed to be godfather to their third child, a daughter born in 1946.

OPPOSITE
Lucie and Raymond's long and happy marriage was founded on the bedrock of their shared beliefs and values.

Lucie became a teacher while Raymond worked as a civil engineer. Then, in 1972, Klaus Barbie was arrested in Bolivia and brought back to be tried in 1987. As part of his testimony, he claimed that it was Raymond who had betrayed Jean Moulin by passing on details of the meeting in the doctor's surgery to the Germans. Lucie and Raymond were outraged, and when the allegations were repeated in a book published in 1997, they sued for libel and won. Some historians found inconsistencies in a memoir Lucie had written about their wartime experiences, but she argued that it was produced 40 years after the events in question and thus she could be forgiven for getting a few dates wrong. It seems clear that Barbie was lying and that he accused Raymond Aubrac because of the contempt he had for his communist beliefs. There is no doubt at all about the value of the work Lucie and Raymond did for the Resistance. When Raymond died in 2012, French president François Hollande said, "In our darkest times, he was, with Lucie Aubrac, among the righteous, who found, in themselves and in the universal values of our Republic, the strength to resist Nazi barbarism."

"In life, there are only three or four fundamental decisions to make. The rest is just luck."

Raymond always said the decision he was most proud of was when he chose Lucie as his partner. They were in it together all the way. "In life," he said, "there are only three or four fundamental decisions to make. The rest is just luck."

IDENTITY CARD

HEDLEY RANFORD NASH
NAME

CANADIAN
NATIONALITY

JANUARY 13, 1912
DOB

PRIVATE
ROLE

ROYAL CANADIAN ELECTRICAL AND MECHANICAL ENGINEERS AND ROYAL CANADIAN ARMY SERVICE CORPS
ORGANIZATION

DEVORAH "DORRIT" BUSS AVROHOM HACKER
NAME

AUSTRIAN
NATIONALITY

OCTOBER 30, 1923
DOB

Hedley & Dorrit Nash

CANADIAN WIVES' BUREAU - CIVILIAN REPATRIATION SECTION

DRAFT REPAT / 77

SHEET NO : 23

MILITARY DISTRICT NO : 7

PAGE NO : 2

PPC NO	REGT NO RANK & INTS	WIFE'S NAME	CHILDRENS' NAMES	AGES	ADDRESS IN U K	ADDRESS IN CANADA
5368	E0185 Gnr BH	JOHNSON Jean M				
4188	G50415 L/Cpl MN	KIERSTEAD Mary D			169 Coperscope Rd Beckenham Kent	Mr & Mrs H Johnson (Parents/Law) Tide Head NB
732	C14100 Gnr W	KINGSTON Catherine	Catherine B	4m	1 Lawson Place Dundee Scotland	Mr Malcolm N Kierstead (Husband) c/o Cameron Coal's Queens County NB
92	G1143 Tpr CBR	KNOX Sarah			11 Bridge St Longriggend Lanarkshire	Mrs George Kingston (M/L) Black River Rd St John NB
39	G27249 Sgt BR	KYLE Barbara C	Dora S Kenneth D	4y4m 2y7m	61 Langside Ave Viewpark Uddingstone Glasgow	Mrs HE Knox (M/L) 303 Rockland Rd St John NB
1	G18582 Pte GC	LANE Violet DK			102 The Glade Old Coulsdon Surrey	Mrs Dan Kyle (M/L) Sussex NB
	G6099 Gnr BF	MACDONALD Kathleen	Vivienne J	4m	15 Ringwood Rd Reading Berks	Mrs F Gayton 51 Pearl St Moncton NB
	A107814 Cpl RH	MURRAY Olga			64 Hawthorne St Wilmslow Cheshire	Mr WF MacDonald (F/L) St Stephen NB
	C23879 Pte HR	NASH Dorrit	Diane S	5m	14 Gothe St Ardwick Manchester 12 Lancs	Mr RH Murray (Husband) Humphreys West Co NB
	G23885 Gnr NB	PATERSON Helen	Ross A	4m	153 Ledbury Rd London W 11	Mrs A Nash (M/L) Ripples RR #3 Sunbury Co NB
	G4328 Gnr WF	ROSS Zena WR	Valerie P	3m	27 Allander St Possil Park Glasgow	Mr JS Paterson (F/L) Centreville Carleton
	G27529 Pte RV	RUSSELL			19 Erskine Rd	

10273

Hedley volunteered for the Canadian Army in 1942, not because of a patriotic spirit, but simply in order to put food on the table...

ABOVE
Hedley in London, 1944. According to his captain, he was considered a "cheerful, friendly man."

Hedley and Dorrit had the odds stacked against them, with different skin colors, religions, nationalities, and backgrounds, but it seemed auspicious that they won a dance contest on their very first date and before long they both knew they were falling for each other.

Hedley's family was dirt poor. He grew up in Lakeville Corner, about 20 miles east of Fredericton, New Brunswick, one of ten brothers and two sisters all living in a tiny shack in the midst of a farming community. The family was descended from Black Loyalists, who had fought with the British during the American Revolutionary War (1775–83). Hedley also had some Maliseet Indian ancestors on his mother's side. At the age of 11, Hedley left school to work on a farm and earn money to help support the family, so he was only able to complete the fifth grade. Over the next 19 years, he took seasonal farm work, labored as a coal miner, and helped out as a mechanic in his uncle's garage, but had no further education. Hedley volunteered for the Canadian Army in 1942, not because of a patriotic spirit, but simply in order to put food on the table and perhaps raise his standard of living.

By contrast, Dorrit Hacker grew up in a comfortable house in Vienna with her upper-middle-class Jewish parents. She was an only child, raised on Mozart, who often attended the opera and wanted for nothing. She was doing well at school when suddenly, at the age of nine, she was told Jewish children were no longer welcome and instantly the girls who had been her closest friends stopped talking to her. Dorrit was distressed and had no idea what was going on, because her parents

BELOW
Dorrit and her mother in Vienna, c.1933, before their world fell apart.

ABOVE
Jewish businesses in Magdeburg, Germany, after Kristallnacht (the Night of Broken Glass), November 9–10, 1938.

did their best to protect her from the growing anti-Semitism in Austria. Further misfortune struck at the age of ten when she succumbed to encephalitis, which caused a permanent droop on one side of her face. After German troops marched into the country in the 1938 Anschluss (union), Dorrit's parents realized that their lives could be in danger and her father Alfons, an accountant, sailed to Palestine to try to establish a home for them there. Dorrit and her mother waited for him to send for them, but he found it difficult to get a work permit because, despite all his lofty qualifications, he didn't speak Hebrew.

The night of November 9, 1938, has gone down in infamy as the Kristallnacht, when Jewish businesses were smashed and burned, and thousands of Jews were rounded up and taken to camps. On November 10th, Dorrit and her mother went to the market; upon returning, some 15 or 20 minutes later, they found that all the people in their entirely Jewish neighborhood had vanished. It was now all too clear that they could no longer wait for word from Palestine, but it was hard to get permits to live anywhere outside of Germany. Nevertheless, Dorrit's mother, Irma, managed to obtain permission to work as a domestic in London and applied to get Dorrit a place on the newly formed Kindertransport,

THE KINDERTRANSPORT

On November 15, 1938, five days after the mass arrests of Kristallnacht, British Jewish leaders urged the prime minister Neville Chamberlain to do something to save Jewish children on the Continent. A bill was quickly passed waiving entry requirements for children under the age of 17 who were thought to be in danger at home, and making arrangements for them to cross to Britain. The first party of 200 children from Berlin and Hamburg arrived on December 2nd. Each child was allowed just one small suitcase and less than ten marks in cash, and upon arrival they were put into children's homes or foster placements. The last Kindertransport set sail from Holland on May 14, 1940, as Nazi troops marched into the country. Over a period of 17 months, nearly 10,000 children were brought to Britain from Germany, Austria, Czechoslovakia, and Poland; many of them would be the only members of their families to survive the war.

London child 7057 4121

This document of identity is issued with the approval of His Majesty's Government in the United Kingdom to young persons to be admitted to the United Kingdom for educational purposes under the care of the Inter-Aid Committee for children.

THIS DOCUMENT REQUIRES NO VISA.

PERSONAL PARTICULARS.

Name HACKER DORRIT

Sex F. Date of Birth 30.10.23

Place VIENNA

Full Names and Address of Parents

HACKER ALFONS + IRMA.

89. OBERE DONAUSTR

VIENNA

BACKGROUND
Scared, missing their families, and with no idea what to expect, refugee children traveled to London by train and boat on the Kindertransport.

LEFT
Dorrit's identification card. Each child transported required one.

Fürsorge-Zentrale der isr. Kultusgemeinde Wien

Kleider (Effekten) -Verzeichnis
des Kindes:

Name: Dorrit Hacker geboren: 30 Oktober 1923
Adresse: [illegible]

Gegenstand:	Zahl	Gegenstand	Zahl
Ganze ~~Anzüge~~ oder Kleider	10	Taschentücher	38
Mantel	2	Mütze u. Hüte	6
Regenmantel	1	Badeanzug	1
Pullower	4	Kamm und Bürste, je	1
~~Weste~~ Blusen	7	Zahnbürste	2
Hosen Röcke	3	Seife	2
Jacken	5	Zahnpasta	1
Taghemden	14	Wäschesack	1
Nachthemden	10	Tefillah	1
Pyjamas	2	[illegible] ~~Schuhbänder~~	3
Leibchen ~~Hemdhosen~~	3	Schreibpapier od. Postkarten, möglichst mit Adressen	10
Unterhosen	12	Sonstiges [illegible]	6
Schürzen	5	[illegible]	6
Schuhe [illegible]	4	[illegible]	
Hausschuhe	2	[illegible]	
Strümpfe	17	[illegible]	
Socken	3	[illegible]	
Handschuhe u. [illegible]	4	[illegible]	

Sämtliche Effekten müssen in gutem Zustand und deutlich sichtbar mit Initialien gezeichnet sein; für ungezeichnete Sachen wird keine Verantwortung übernommen. Dieses Verzeichnis ist genau ausgefüllt und unterzeichnet den Reiseeffekten beizulegen.

Für die Richtigkeit (Unterschrift der Mutter): Sabine Hacker

Wien, am [illegible] 1939 Grossmutter u. Vormund.

ABOVE
Before leaving Austria, Dorrit had to fill out this form listing all of her belongings. At the bottom is the signature of her grandmother, Sabine Hacker, whom Dorrit would never see or hear from again.

established to rescue unaccompanied Jewish children from Central Europe. Irma then traveled ahead to London, leaving Dorrit in Vienna with her paternal grandmother.

It must have been terrifying for 15-year-old Dorrit to take the train and the boat across to London, particularly as she spoke no English. On arrival she was placed in a Jewish children's refugee home, where she stayed until her mother managed to track her down. Irma had found work as a live-in servant in a wealthy household and also persuaded them to employ Dorrit, claiming they were sisters. Back home in Vienna, they'd employed a domestic themselves and knew very little about cleaning, but somehow they coped with the work. Dorrit briefly attended school in London in order to learn some English, but her mother withdrew her as soon as she heard that students were caned by the headmaster for minor offenses. Instead, Dorrit had to learn English on the job, but she was bright and she picked it up quickly.

Still, Dorrit and her mother were anxious. They had received no word from Dorrit's father since he had left for Palestine. They were worried about relatives back home in Austria. Although they spoke English, their heavy Austrian accents sounded German to the British, and thus they were forever having to explain their situation. They also worried that the anti-Jewish sentiment sweeping the continent would follow them to London and nowhere would be safe. It was a nerve-racking time all around.

London in Wartime

Hedley did his basic army training in New Brunswick and worked as a truck driver for the Army Service Corps. In September 1943, he was brought to London to work in an engineering workshop, where he trained to be an electric-light plant operator. Perhaps because he was already 30 years old, he wasn't sent out to take part in the action, but was lucky enough to get the jobs he did, having joined up so late as an unskilled recruit.

"I had to lay on my back with a burning hot blowtorch, tacking together large pieces of metal while outside...bombs were being dropped all around."

When war was declared, Dorrit was determined to do her part for the war effort and she tried to volunteer for the Auxiliary Territorial Service (the Women's Army). But at only 15 and a half years old, she was 18 months too young, and was referred instead to a war training center in Hounslow, on the outskirts of London, where she spent six months being trained in sheet-metal work and gas welding. Her first job was welding tailpipes for fighter planes, and she wrote in her diary, "I had to lay on my back with a burning hot blowtorch, tacking together large pieces of metal while outside the air raid sirens were howling and bombs were being dropped all around."

She and her mother were terrified of the bombs. Once they saw a plane crash into a building, and Dorrit vowed never to fly for as long as she lived. She made the same resolution about elevators after getting stuck in one during an air raid when the power was cut, and she was powerless as she watched another passenger suffer a heart attack and die in front of her.

Dorrit and her mother were devastated when word reached them that both of Dorrit's grandmothers had been rounded up and taken to camps, along with all the other Jews who had stayed behind in Austria. An uncle was taken as well, and yet another uncle hanged himself to avoid the same fate. Irma wept over the family photographs she had managed to bring with her. They still had no idea where Dorrit's father was, and they feared the worst.

No matter how bad the news, however, Dorrit was a teenager during the war and wanted to enjoy herself, so in her time off work she went with her girlfriends to dance halls or to see films. She changed jobs and got work as a cashier in a servicemen's canteen, and it was there that a Canadian serviceman began to flirt with her one Friday night. He told her there was a dance contest at the nearby Club Trocadero, with a chicken as the prize for the winning couple, and he asked if she would be his partner. At first Dorrit refused because she didn't know him, but Hedley was a handsome, charming man and the thought of a chicken to supplement her meager wartime rations was irresistible.

Dorrit had always been a keen dancer and it turned out that Hedley was pretty nifty on his feet, too. As they danced the jitterbug, the jive, and the foxtrot, the dance floor cleared and people stood watching. At the end of the evening, the prize was theirs. Hedley let her take it home to her mother, because as a Canadian serviceman he was well fed. But the dance contests that were common at that time gave him an excellent excuse to invite her to come dancing with him again.

Dorrit had dated a few other men, but soon she began seeing Hedley exclusively. One thing they had in common was that they were both outsiders, and after the first few dates it became clear that things were getting serious. "You do know I'm Jewish, don't you?" she asked, feeling it was only fair to warn him. He grinned and replied, "I don't care. I love you. Besides, you do know I'm black, don't you?" "I don't care, either," she replied.

BELOW
Showing off their moves: American servicemen at the Rainbow Club near Piccadilly Circus, London, January 27 1945.

Life in Canada

When Dorrit announced in the spring of 1945 that Hedley had asked her to marry him, her mother tried to talk her out of it. Dorrit was barely 21 years old, Hedley was black and non-Jewish, and he would probably want to take her only daughter back to Canada. She argued against the match, but Dorrit would not be swayed. In June 1945, a civil ceremony was performed in London, making them man and wife. A friend of Hedley's was one of the witnesses and his future mother-in-law, Irma, was the other. A shock awaited them when they signed the marriage register. Hedley had told Dorrit he was 21, like her, but in the register his age was recorded as 33—a full 12 years older. Irma was furious about the deception, but Dorrit shrugged it off. Age doesn't matter when you are in love.

ABOVE
Dorrit's mother, Irma, carefully cut Hedley's image off this picture of Dorrit with her new baby Diane. Irma found it hard to accept the relationship.

There was good news at last when they heard that Dorrit's father was alive and well, having survived the war in Palestine. He came to London in the summer of 1946 to find that his little daughter had married and was herself the mother of a baby girl called Diane. At the same time, they learned that other relatives had not been so fortunate; nothing was ever discovered as to the fate of Dorrit's grandmothers and the uncle who had been sent to the concentration camps.

Hedley was repatriated to Canada with his military comrades in September 1946. He was followed by Dorrit, who sailed out on the *Empire Brent* in October, along with hundreds of other war brides, on one of the special sailings arranged by the Red Cross. She came ashore in Halifax with her five-month-old daughter and caught a train to Fredericton to be reunited with her husband. It was then that Hedley's second falsehood came to light. He had told Dorrit that he owned a chain of garages and led her to believe they would have a comfortable lifestyle, but reality became clear when she arrived at the tiny shack where Hedley's parents lived with all his siblings. It was November and already the winter was unbelievably cold, with snow thick on the ground. There was no electricity, so Dorrit had to find her way at night using oil lamps. There was no indoor plumbing and the toilet was some distance away from the house, so a call of nature meant donning jackets and overshoes to plod through the snow. Dorrit was stunned by her change in circumstances, but stuck in a foreign land she had no recourse but to make the best of it. Fortunately, her husband's large family was kind and welcoming.

In March 1947, after a winter staying with the in-laws, Hedley and Dorrit were able to rent a house of their own in Fredericton. The house had an indoor toilet and the luxury of hot running water. Hedley got work as a laborer, and then as a piece worker in the Chestnut Canoe Company, but despite working long hours, he earned very little. Dorrit became expert at producing meals

WAR BRIDE CROSSINGS

The end of the war and the subsequent repatriation of troops meant that hundreds of thousands of couples, many of them with young children, were separated. The Red Cross stepped in to look after the women and children left behind, to counsel them in preparation for life overseas, organize paperwork, arrange war bride sailings, and accompany them on the journey to their new homes. In some cases, they provided ongoing help for years after the war, including assistance for women who became too homesick and decided to return to their countries of origin because they couldn't adjust to life in a new land. The first official sailing of a war bride ship was in January 1946, when the SS *Argentina* took 452 women from Southampton to New York, to be met by the mayor, a band playing, and 200 journalists and photographers. War bride sailings continued until 1948, involving hundreds of ships, and were given many slang names, including "The Diaper Run" and "Operation Mother-in-law."

ABOVE
There was a spirit of camaraderie on war bride crossings and many women made lifelong friendships.

out of beans, potatoes, or macaroni along with any meat that was on sale. Two more daughters were born—Denise and Deby—and when the girls were old enough they walked the mile or so to the local school.

Poverty was not the family's only problem. They were the first mixed-race family in Fredericton, living in a white community, and they encountered a certain amount of prejudice. Although Dorrit and Hedley had many friends and often entertained them at the family home, invitations were not returned because white neighbors didn't want a black man in their house. Dorrit attended events at the local synagogue, but her husband was discouraged by the Jewish community from accompanying her. The girls were told they couldn't swim in certain swimming pools or take part in athletic events; there were some places that people of color could not go. All the same, Hedley and Dorrit's daughters did extremely well at school—an achievement that astounded Dorrit, who was unable to help them with homework since her own academic education had been so curtailed.

... Hedley and Dorrit remained in love throughout 57 years of marriage, and retained their love of dancing.

ABOVE
Dorrit and Hedley: dancing brought them together and they never missed a chance to have a twirl.

Dorrit's mother, Irma, went back to Vienna sporadically to be with Alfons, but she was hurt by his lack of support during wartime and spent more and more time with her daughter and grandchildren in Canada. Although she never forgave Hedley for the lies about his age and his circumstances, she couldn't contemplate losing touch with her only child and, after Alfons died, she came to live in Canada.

Despite all the challenges and the world of difference between them, Hedley and Dorrit remained in love throughout 57 years of marriage—and both retained their love of dancing. At social events—including their daughters' weddings—they got up to jive or jitterbug, just as they had back in wartime, and they always cleared the floor.

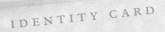

IDENTITY CARD

ROY OSCAR SATHER
NAME

AMERICAN
NATIONALITY

JULY 17, 1917
DOB

MAJOR
ROLE

468TH BOMBARDMENT GROUP
ORGANIZATION

PAULINE "PILL" ADDIE DENMAN
NAME

AMERICAN
NATIONALITY

DECEMBER 1920
DOB

LIEUTENANT
ROLE

ARMY NURSE CORPS
ORGANIZATION

Roy Sather & Pill Denman

ABOVE
Pauline and Roy saw each other three times a day on Tinian. They spent their days going to the beach, playing games, talking—and falling in love.

It was an idyllic romance on a tropical island between two people who simply clicked. "Practice signing Mrs. Roy O. Sather," Roy told Pill the day before she was shipped off to Japan to finish her tour of duty. She had no doubt that they would spend the rest of their lives together.

By the summer of 1945, Roy had already endured a long, tough war. After studying electrical engineering at Wayne State University, he had signed up for the Air Corps and was sent to a training camp in Salina, Kansas, where he learned to fly fighter-bombers. In 1941, he got a job as a flight instructor and was sent for a tour of duty in Northern Ireland. In May 1943, he joined the newly formed 468th Bombardment Group, the first to fly high-altitude B-29 aircraft on overseas missions. These were brand new planes with lots of technical issues to be resolved before they were sent to Calcutta, India in March/April 1944, for use in the China–Burma–India theater. Their initial missions involved flying "over the hump"—the Himalayas—to take fuel to an advanced base in Szechuan province in China. Then on June 5, 1944, the 468th flew their first bombing mission over Bangkok, Thailand, before later attacking military targets in Japan. Roy was a radar operator—"a near-genius, the best in the business," according to his commanding officer. He flew 17 successful missions altogether.

ABOVE
Roy began his army career as a lieutenant in Northern Ireland.

BELOW
B-29s of the 468th Group dropping their payloads over Rangoon in Burma.

By the end of 1944, the 468th had the best operational record of the four B-29 bomb groups then in existence, for which they were rewarded with the title "The General Billy Mitchell Group" (after the man credited with creating the United States Air Force). The work was undoubtedly challenging, as the B-29s were still prone to technical problems, and every mission was a trial of nerves lasting between 16 and 21 hours before they were safely back at base. "I used to fly until I found out how dangerous it was," Roy quipped to friends, typically making light of the very real peril he had been in.

In May 1945, the 468th were relocated to Tinian, one of the Mariana Islands southeast of Japan, which had been liberated from Japanese occupation the previous summer. One end of the island was completely fenced off for a top-secret mission involving B-29s, but few knew precisely what that might involve. All they knew was that the boundary was guarded and that something big was going on.

FLYING THE HUMP

China had been at war with Japan since 1937, and the American strategy in this conflict was to supply aid to the Chinese to help them fight back. Once Burma had fallen to Japan in May 1942, this could only be done by air from India. From July 1942 until November 1945, 650,000 tons of supplies were flown over "the hump" amid treacherous flying conditions. There were steep ascents, as they rose from sea level and had to clear ridges of up to 16,000 feet; winds could gust at up to 200 mph, causing severe turbulence; and the planes would often either overheat or get iced up at altitude. Mechanical failure was common and spare parts were hard to come by—and there was also the added danger of attack by Japanese fighter planes. At least 509 planes were lost flying "the hump," with 1,314 air crew members killed, while approximately 1,200 men were rescued after crashing. Roy wasn't joking when he said flying was dangerous!

Life was more relaxed on Tinian than it had been in Calcutta, with fewer missions to fly, and Roy enjoyed going to the beach and exploring the island in a jeep borrowed from the motor pool. There were dances at the officers' clubs and one night he spotted an attractive girl with blonde hair and glasses and he thought she looked fun. He contrived an introduction and found out that her name was Pill (short for Pauline) and she was a nurse. They started chatting, then something happened that neither had expected: there was such an intense, immediate attraction between them that the rest of the world faded into the background. From then on, for the remainder of their time on Tinian, they only had eyes for each other.

...there was such an intense, immediate attraction between them that the rest of the world faded into the background.

Love in the Tropics

When she graduated from high school in Delmar, New York, Pill Denman had no idea what she wanted to do with her life. Her friend Cookie announced she was going into nursing, and Pill thought, "Why not?" She soon found she enjoyed the job and after earning her RN in 1943, she decided to join the army to do her part for the war effort. Her first assignment was working night shifts from 6:00 p.m. to 6:00 a.m. on an obstetrics ward in Fort Monmouth, New Jersey, and after a few months of that she signed up for overseas service. She hoped to be sent to Europe, and packed her warmest clothes, but the war in Europe was coming to an end just as she arrived for training at Camp Kilmer, New Jersey; she was told she would need summer clothes, since her next stop would be the Pacific. There was just time to learn about the symptoms of malaria before she and the other volunteers were sent by train to Seattle, Washington, where they would embark. They didn't know where they were going when they set sail on July 17, 1945, but the speculation was excitement enough.

Their ship docked at Tinian Island in the Marianas and the girls were shown to Quonset (prefabricated steel) huts on the island's east side, where they would sleep 25 or 30 to a room and share an outdoor latrine. There wasn't any nursing to do, so after they had finished a few chores, their days were their own. Pill had only been

OPPOSITE
Flying "the hump" was treacherous, but with breathtaking views of the Himalayas.

there a week when she met Roy, and although she was fairly casual in her letters home to her parents, she began to mention him in every one: "He's an awfully nice fellow ... honest and faithful and has a lot of grey matter under his thinning red hair … I think an awful lot of him." In fact, she was soon smitten and didn't have eyes for anyone else, as she and Roy spent all their free time together.

Roy slept in a tent on the west of the island where all the officers were based, but every morning after breakfast he would drive the four miles over to Pill's hut. In the hours they were apart they used to write letters to each other, so the first thing they did was read the letters each had written in bed the night before. They played games of cribbage and Sink (a form of Battleship), they filled out crossword puzzles, which both enjoyed, and the whole time they talked—about his father who had died in World War I, soon after he was born; about her older sister, Marjorie, who was a secretary; about his time as a cross-country running champion; about the experiences she'd had as a nurse. Their conversation was one long stream that never ran out—except when they stopped for passionate kisses.

In the afternoons, they generally went to the beach to swim and goof around in the sand, and every evening after dinner they went out: to a drive-in movie, dancing, or for rum and cokes at one of the officers' clubs (their favorite was the Dreamboat, which had the great luxury of an indoor toilet). It should have been perfect, but Roy had a secret weighing on his conscience. One day he asked Pill out for a long walk and began, hesitantly, to tell her about a friend of his who had a problem. The friend, he said, was engaged to a girl called Irene, but he wasn't in love with her and now he had fallen for a nurse on Tinian. What should he do? Pill could guess from the nervous way he spoke that he was talking about himself and she answered carefully. She said his friend should go back to the United States and see his fiancée again before making any final decisions. That way he would know for sure if he were doing the right thing. Roy confessed to Pill that it was him and showed her photos of Irene. "But I want to be with you," he said. "You're the one I love." There was such emotion in his voice that she knew for sure he meant every word.

BELOW
Roy with Irene Markham, his fiancée before the war.

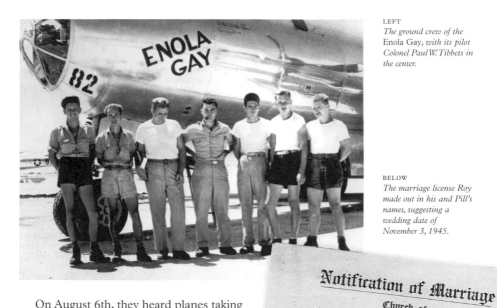

LEFT
The ground crew of the Enola Gay, *with its pilot Colonel Paul W. Tibbets in the center.*

BELOW
The marriage license Roy made out in his and Pill's names, suggesting a wedding date of November 3, 1945.

On August 6th, they heard planes taking off from the north end of the island where the secret base was located, and heard later that the flight had included a plane called *Enola Gay*, which had dropped a very special kind of bomb. Roy was curious but Pill didn't give it much thought at the time. Then on August 9th, another bomb was dropped, and on the 15th came news that Japan had surrendered (see p185). The war was over, bringing with it huge relief that Roy and his comrades wouldn't have to risk their lives any more. There were special celebrations on Tinian that night, and Roy and Pill sat holding hands on the terrace of the Dreamboat Club, watching the planes return from their final missions.

Notification of Marriage

Church of GENERAL BILLY MITCHELL GROUP
TINIAN ISLAND – MARIANAS.

Name PAULINE A. DENMAN

Residence NURSES' STOCKADE – 96TH STREET

Satherized: ~~Baptised~~ 7 AUGUST 1945

on the 7TH day of AUGUST 1945

Parents MR & MRS RALPH DENMAN
DELMAR, NEW YORK

Married to ROY OSCAR SATHER Age 28

Parents YES, OF COURSE!

on the 3RD day of NOVEMBER 1945

With Witnesses COL JIM
COL SHOES

By the Rev. CHAPLAIN GUNN PASTOR

Dated 3RD NOVEMBER, 1945 DELEGATE

THE MCCOY COMPANY, SAN FRANCISCO, CALIF.

A Sad Goodbye

Military personnel came and went from Tinian all the time. Roy had come to the end of his tour and could have gone home soon after VJ Day, but Pill was committed to working for six months after the end of the war, so he kept negotiating extensions simply so that he could stay with her. All the time things were getting more serious between them. He took her for lunch in the officers' mess and introduced her to his commanding officer, Colonel Jim Edmundson. One day he presented her with a marriage license he had made out in their names, suggesting a wedding date of November 3rd. He gave her his engraved chain-link bracelet and his Air Force dog tag. And all the time he told her how much he loved her, though she knew he did, and she explained that she loved him, too. Everything about it felt completely right, as if it had always been meant to be.

Then Pill was told that she would soon be sent to Japan to nurse American troops stationed there. It broke her heart to think of leaving Roy, but he reassured her that he would write to her twice a day, and that she just had to get through the final months of her service so that they could then be reunited. On October 19th, the day she left, as there were no jewelry stores on Tinian where he could buy her a ring, he gave her his gold, engraved Parker 51 pen and pencil set as what he called "an engagement present," and told her to practice writing "Mrs." before the name on that pen. He didn't get down on bended knee but, all the same, this proposal was the only thing that comforted Pill as her ship set sail across the Pacific.

OPPOSITE
The mushroom cloud above Nagasaki on August 8, 1945, rose more than 60,000 feet into the air.

True to his word, Roy wrote twice a day, sending news of their friends on Tinian and telling her how much he missed her. The mail wasn't always regular, so on November 15th she received fourteen letters from him all on one day, while on other days she received nothing at all. Pill missed him terribly but soon settled to her life in Japan. There were no gunshot wounds or bomb-blast injuries to deal with; the men she was nursing had nothing more serious than a hernia or appendicitis. She visited Hiroshima and found a barren landscape of nothing but ashes; shocked, she wrote

BELOW
Roy's engraved pen and pencil set, which he gave to Pill as an engagement present since there were no jewelry shops on Tinian.

HIROSHIMA & NAGASAKI

Colonel Paul W. Tibbets entered the history books on August 6, 1945, when he flew the *Enola Gay* (named after his mother) to Hiroshima and dropped the bomb known as "Little Boy." It was the first time an atomic bomb had been unleashed on the world; Tibbets described the cloud that arose as "boiling up, mushrooming, terrible, and incredibly tall," but that doesn't begin to describe the horror on the ground. Approximately 70,000 people (mostly civilians) were killed that day alone, while another 140,000 would die in the months and years afterward from the effects of radiation. Still, Emperor Hirohito procrastinated over the terms of Japan's surrender, so on August 9th, the US Government felt it necessary to send a second mission to drop a similar bomb on Nagasaki. This killed between 60,000 and 80,000 people, roughly half of them on the first day. President Truman claimed that the use of atomic bombs prevented the loss of a further half a million US lives by bringing the war to a rapid end, but the ethical debate continues.

home, "It is impossible to put into words the destruction caused by that one small powerful bomb."

"*It is impossible to put into words the destruction caused by that one small powerful bomb.*"

Roy wrote that he would be arriving back in the US on December 2nd, and gave her the address at which she should write to him. She sent a letter immediately and carried on writing, but nothing arrived in return. At first she thought there must be some difficulty with the transport of mail to Japan; then she worried he might have had an accident. When both her birthday and Christmas Day came and went without a word, she became seriously alarmed. Still, she continued to write to the address she had been given until, on January 11, 1946, she received a letter with a California postmark. She ripped it open and her heart broke as she read the words. It was a curt note from Roy's mother telling her that on December 20th, he had married his fiancée, Irene, and asking that she stop writing to him. Pill was utterly devastated.

A few days later, she received a letter from Roy himself, which was postmarked December 3rd, but had obviously been delayed in the mail. He wrote of his arrival back in the States, where he found that his mother and Irene had already arranged the wedding, that everything had been booked, and that he felt he had no choice but to go through with it. "Admittedly, I am going into a marriage without love," he went on, before insisting she was better off being rid of him since he didn't know his own mind.

BELOW
One of Roy's letters to Pill once she was in Japan. He wrote twice a day before his return to the States.

LEFT
Pill in 1951, after getting engaged to Cecil Webb, who would be the father of her two children.

Pill didn't reply. She carried on with her work and when her military service finished, she went home and took up work as a private nurse. She didn't blame Roy; she knew him as a man of honor, who wouldn't have wanted to hurt anyone if he could have avoided it, but the abrupt ending of their relationship took her some time to get over. In 1949, she married a man called Leonard Klein, who tragically died three months later of Hodgkin's Disease. In 1951, she married again, this time to Cecil Webb, with whom she had two children.

Roy continued to work for the Air Force until 1958, then taught electrical and computer engineering at Wayne State University, his old alma mater. He and Irene had four children and stayed together until his death in 1994.

There were many whirlwind romances like Roy and Pill's; the intensity of war led to quick attachments and relationships flowered. No matter how short-lived, they are not diminished for having blazed brightly, but only briefly, before being snuffed out by the realities of ordinary life back home.

Index

A

Aboriginal Australians *85*
all-black/African-American units *47, 49, 85*
Anderson, William & Kathleen *32–43*
Andrews Sisters, the *115*
Armstrong, Louis *109, 115*
Aubrac, Raymond & Lucie *152–63*
Auschwitz *18, 53, 162*
Auxiliary Territorial Service (ATS) *73, 75, 171*

B

B-29s *179, 180*
Bader, Douglas *39, 43*
Bancroft, Mary *116–27*
Barbie, Klaus *156, 159, 160, 161, 163*
Barron, Clarence *119*
Bate, Vera *26*
black market *61, 157*
Bletchley Park *16, 123*
Blitz, the *11, 95, 144*
Blitzkrieg *10*
Bloch, Denise *78–9*
Boyington, Pappy *134, 136*
Braun, Wernher von *66*
Brauny, Erhard *108*
Britain, Battle of *11, 12*
Brooke, General Sir Alan *14*
Buchenwald *51*
Bulge, Battle of the *17*

C

Capel, Arthur "Boy" *23*
Central Intelligence Agency (CIA) *127*
Chamberlain, Neville *9, 10, 11, 169*
Chanel, Coco *20–31*
Churchill, Winston *10, 11, 12, 14, 18, 26, 28, 29, 77, 99*
codes and code breakers *16, 123*
Cold War *19*
Colditz *37–8, 39–41*
escape attempts *39–40, 42*
collaborators *27, 157, 162*
computer art *67*
concentration camps *18, 30, 51, 53, 63, 78, 108, 109, 150, 162, 171, 173*
Cooper, Tommy *115*

D

D-Day landings *16, 17, 40, 41, 48, 50, 61–3, 99, 144, 145, 156*
Dachau *150*
de Gaulle, Charles *28, 74, 157, 158, 162*
Denman, Pill *176–87*
Dincklage, Hans von *20–31*
Dora-Mittelbau *53, 108*
Dulles, Allen *116–27*
Dunkirk evacuation *10–11, 36, 37*

E

Early, Major Charity Adams *53*
Eisenhower, David *103*
Eisenhower, Dwight D. *13, 16, 17, 62, 92–103*
Eisenhower, John S.D. *53, 100*
Eisenhower, Mamie *96, 99, 100, 101, 103*
El Alamein, Battle of *13, 74, 98*
Enigma code breakers *16, 123*
entertaining the troops *109, 115*

F

First Nation Canadians *83, 85, 87, 88, 90–1, 167*
flying "the hump" *179, 180*
Franco, Francisco *9*
Frank, Hans *30*
Free French forces *72, 74*

G

Gardelegen massacre *108, 109*
Gelenne, Elly *61, 63, 65*
"Germany First" policy *14–15*
Gisevius, Hans Bernd *124–5, 127*
Goebbels, Josef *17, 24, 25*
Göring, Hermann *11, 25, 30, 127*
Grable, Betty *115*
Guadalcanal *133–4, 136*
Guitry, Sacha *27*

H

Haedrich, Marcel *31*
Hall, Virginia *77*
Henry, Desmond Paul and Louisa *56–67*
Hiroshima *19, 184, 185, 186*
Hitler, Adolph *8–9, 10, 11, 12, 13, 14, 41, 121*
assassination plot *125*
final days *18, 19*
Ho Chi Minh *162*
Hollande, François *163*
Hope, Bob *115*
Howerd, Frankie *115*

I

indigenous peoples *85*

J

Jung, Carl *120*

K

Kennedy, John F. *126, 127, 134, 135*

Kindertransport *168–70*
Klarsfeld, Beate *161*
Kolbe, Fritz *124*
Kristallnacht *168, 169*

L

Lifar, Serge *27*
Lowry, L.S. *67*
Luxembourg, Rosa *25*
Lynn, Vera *115*

M

Mathausen *53*
medals *79, 138*
Miller, Merle *102*
Molotov, Vyacheslav *9*
Monte Cassino *110*
Montgomery, General Bernard *13, 16, 97, 98*
Moore, Bill & Norma Kay *44–55*
Moulin, Jean *158, 159, 160, 163*
Mulberries *16, 145*
Mussolini, Benito *9, 18, 19, 35, 86, 121*

N

Nagasaki *19, 185*
Nash, Hedley & Dorrit *164–75*
Native Americans *85, 123*
Neave, Airey *42*
New Zealand *131–3, 137–9*
Normandy landings *see* D-Day landings
North Africa *12–13, 16, 72, 74, 96, 97, 110*
El Alamein *13, 74, 98*
Norwalk, Bob & Rosie *140–51*
nuclear weapons *19, 183, 185*
Nuremberg Trials *30, 127*

O

Office of Strategic Services (OSS) *121–2, 127*

P

Pacific, war in *14–15, 131, 133–7*
Patton, General *53, 97, 98*
Paul, Charley & Jean *80–91*
Pearl Harbour *14, 47, 123, 131*
Pétain, Marshall *27, 74*
Phony War *10*
Piaf, Edith *27*
Poland *9, 10, 18, 30, 143*
prisoners-of-war *37–40, 51, 148*

R

racial segregation *49, 53, 54, 85, 175*
rationing *39, 61*
Ravensbrück *78–9*
Red Ball Express *50–1, 53*
Red Cross *37, 39, 41, 126, 137, 145–7, 148, 150, 156, 174*
Resistance, the *27, 29, 50, 61, 76–7, 79, 124, 156–60, 162, 163*
Ribbentrop, Joachim von *9, 25, 30*
Rolfe, Lilian *78–9*
Rommel, General Erwin *12, 13, 16, 74, 75*
Roosevelt, Franklin D. *14, 99*

S

Sachsenhausen *18*
Sansom, Odette *77*
Sather, Roy *176–87*
Schellenberg, Walter *26, 28, 30*
Schillinger, Hans *29*
Schulze-Gaevernitz, Gero von *124*
Sicily *84, 86, 98, 110*
Skarbek, Krystyna *77*
Special Operations Executive (SOE) *75–6, 77*
Stalingrad, Battle of *13*
Stauffenberg, Claus von *125*
Stern Gang *110*
Summersby, Kay *92–103*
Szabo, Étienne & Violette *68–79*

T

Thiele, Gerhard *108*
Truman, Harry *102, 185*
Turing, Alan *123*
Turner, Hudson & Betty *128–39*

V

V-1/V-2 rockets *61, 63, 64, 66, 125, 145–6*
Vichy government *24, 74*

W

Wake, Nancy *77*
war brides *65, 86–7, 90, 113, 138–9, 173, 174*
war crimes trials *30, 43, 127, 161, 162*
Williams, Roger & Rosemarie *104–15*
Windsor, Duke and Duchess of *28–9*
Wolff, Karl *126*

ACKNOWLEDGMENTS

Warm thanks to Colin Salter, who helped to track down some of the stories, to Luisa Stucchi for her wonderful BBC Radio 4 documentary about war brides, and to Melynda Jarratt, who has been unfailingly generous with her time and contacts. I recommend her books *Captured Hearts* and *War Brides*, and her website www.canadianwarbrides.com for everything to do with the Canadian war bride experience.

I'm also extremely grateful to the individual family members who helped me to research the stories:

Anderson: Stuart and Antony Anderson gave me lengthy interviews and supplied lots of wonderful pictures. Many thanks to them.

Denman: Pauline Webb chatted to me on the phone about her wartime romance, and I was also able to read her diaries from the time in her book *Letters from Tinian 1945*. Thanks also to her daughter Debra Rogers for helping me to make contact.

Henry: I am indebted to Elaine O'Hanrahan for all her meticulous help in compiling her parents' story.

Moore: thanks to Christopher Paul Moore for answering my questions about his parents. I recommend his excellent book *Fighting for America* for everything to do with the experience of being black in the military. Thanks also to Nancy Lipscomb and Kim Yancy for helping me to make contact with him.

Nash: Deby Nash kindly talked me through her parents' lives and answered all my follow-up queries, while Melynda Jarratt introduced us and sent photographs.

Norwalk: thanks to Tom and Martha Norwalk for talking to me; I highly recommend their mother's book *Dearest Ones* about her experiences in wartime England.

Paul: thanks to Stewart Paul, Lindsay Paul, Cindy Gaffney, Mary Balfour and my namesake Gill Paul for all their help. It was great to meet Lindsay and Gill when they came to London.

Turner: thanks to Don Moore and his website www.donmooreswartales.com for bringing the story to my attention, and to Elizabeth Skelton, daughter of Hudson and Betty, for filling out the details.

Williams: Julia Williams' blog about her mother-in-law www.storiesfromagedmil.blogspot.co.uk was my starting point, and I'm grateful to her for all the additional information and pictures she supplied.

Big thanks to the amazing team at Ivy Press, especially Sophie Collins, Jacqui Sayers and Katie Greenwood.

And thanks as always to Karel Bata for putting up with me.

PICTURE CREDITS

Alexander Turnbull Library, Wellington, New Zealand: *133*, *139*.

Courtesy of Antony Anderson: *32–36*, *40–41*.

Bridgeman Art Library/Bibliotheque des Arts Decoratifs, Paris, France: *25*.

Bundesarchiv/Bild 101III-Alber-178-04A/ Alber, Kurt: *28*; Bild 146-1970-083-42: *168*; Bild *183*-S*69279*: *169*B. CC-BY-SA.

Corbis: *24*, *118*; **Bettmann:** *95*, *97*, *101*B, *126*; **DK Limited:** 2B; DPA: *127*; **Ira Nowinski:** *78*.

Courtesy of Pauline Denman: *176–178*, *179*T, *182*, *183*B, *184*, *186*, *187*.

Getty Images/Denver Post: *124*; **Gamma-Rapho:** *157*, *159*; **Hulton Archive:** *13*, *23*, *74*, *115* (main), *144*; **Keystone:** *77*, *145*; **MPI:** *135*T; **New York Daily News:** *115*T; **Picture Post:** *37*, *172*; **Popperfoto:** *6*, *17*, *19*, *68*T, *71*, *72*, *120*; **SSPL:** *16*, *123*; **Time Life Pictures:** *2*T, *12*, *27*B, *101*T, *108*, *110*, *180*; **Roger-Viollet:** *73*B.

iStockphoto/Senorcampesino: *42*.

From the collection of Melynda Jarratt, www.CanadianWarBrides.com: *164*, *166*, *167*, *170*, *173*, *174*.

Library and Archives Canada: *80*, *84*.

Library of Congress, Washington, D.C.: *11*, *27*T, *87*T, *96*, *98*R, *117*T, *121*, *136*, *138*, world map.

Courtesy of Christopher Moore: *45*, *46*, *51*, *54*T.

Courtesy of Deby Nash: *165*, *175*.

The National Archives and Records Administration (NARA): *8–11*, *14*, *15*, *18*, *30*, *47*, *49*, *50*, *52*, *54*B, *62*B, *66*, *67*, *75*, *85*, *92*T, *94*, *98*L, *99*, *100*, *102*, *103*, *134*, *135*B, *179*B, *185*.

Courtesy of Tom Norwalk: *141–143*, *146*, *147*, *150*, *151*.

Courtesy of Elaine O'Hanrahan: *56–58*, *60*, *61*, *62*T, *63–65*, *67*.

Courtesy of Lyndsey Paul, Cindy Gaffney and Tammy Schloemer: *81*, *83*, *87*B, *88*, *89*, *91*.

Provincial Archives of New Brunswick: *164*B, *164*C, *169*T; **Carleton and York Veterans Association**, MC1325/MS4/90: *82*.

Rama: *152*T.

Rex Features/Anthony Wallace/ Associated Newspapers: *79*; **Collect/ Evening News:** *70*; **Everett Collection:** *92*B; LAPI: *158*; **Morris Raymond/Sipa:** *155*; **Roger-Viollet:** *156*, *160*; **Sipa Press:** *153*, *154*, *163*.

Schlesinger Library, Radcliffe Institute, Harvard University: *116*, *117*B.

Shutterstock/AKaiser: *44*; **Zvonimir Atletic:** *93*B; **R Carner:** *129*; **Jacqui Martin:** *20*B; **Neftali:** *152*B; **Sylvana Rega:** *93*T.

Courtesy of Eiizabeth Skelton: *128*, *130*, *132*.

Swiss Federal Archives/CH- BAR#E*4320*B#*1990*/*266*#*1551**, Bd. *177*, Az. C.*16-01373* P, von Dincklage Hans, *1896*, *1939-1958*: *21*T, *31*.

Courtesy of Tania Szabo, www. violetteszabo.org: *69*, *76*.

Topfoto: *68*B, *73*T, *161*; **Roger-Viollet:** *21*B, *22*.

Courtesy of the University of Texas Libraries, The University of Texas: *131*.

U.S. Air Force: *183*T.

Courtesy of Julia Williams: *104–107*, *109*, *111–114*.

Every effort has been made to acknowledge the pictures used in this publication. We apologize if there are any unintentional omissions.